# INTERNATIONAL JOURNAL ON HUMAN RIGHTS, PEACE AND POLITICS

## DISSENT, DEFIANCE, DISCOURSE

BHAVNA DAHIYA

Made with ♥ on the Notion Press Platform
www.notionpress.com

This journal is dedicated to the unsung heroes of our time—the brave individuals who stand tall in the face of oppression, who dare to dissent when silence is safer, and who fight tirelessly for justice in a world that often turns a blind eye.

We dedicate these pages to the marginalized voices that power structures seek to silence: the indigenous communities defending their ancestral lands, the political prisoners languishing behind bars for speaking truth to power, the refugees seeking dignity in a world that too often denies their humanity.

To the activists risking their lives in the streets of Yangon, the journalists uncovering corruption, the human rights defenders documenting abuses in Gaza, and the environmental warriors battling corporate interests in the Amazon—this journal is your platform, your amplifier, your ally.

We dedicate this work to those who refuse to accept that the world as it is, is the world as it must be. To those who, in the words of Howard Zinn, "can't be neutral on a moving train."

Finally, we dedicate this journal to the next generation of scholars, thinkers, and activists. May these pages inspire you, challenge you, and arm you with the knowledge and conviction to continue the fight for a more just and equitable world.

In solidarity and with unwavering commitment to the struggle for human rights, peace, and justice,

"*The Editorial Board International Journal of Human Rights, Peace and Politics*

*Dissent, Defiance, Discourse* "

# Contents

# FOREWORD

## International Journal on Human Rights, Peace, and Politics

The International Journal on Human Rights, Peace, and Politics is a pioneering publication committed to bridging the gap between scholarly research and real-world impact. Our global journal publishes cutting-edge research that not only advances academic knowledge but also fosters tangible change in society.

*We are dedicated to creating a thriving sanctuary for unfiltered, uncensored dialogue that champions free speech, free expression, and a free press.*

### Vision Statement - "Contribute to the change you wish to see in the world"

Our vision is revolutionary: to champion free speech, no censorship, free expression, and a free press. We believe in creating a world where every voice is heard, and every story is told without fear or restraint.

### Mission Statement - "Uncensored, Unfiltered, Unrivaled"

Our mission is to inspire action, influence policy, and promote social justice through rigorous scholarship and inclusive dialogue. We strive to publish innovative, interdisciplinary research that addresses the most pressing issues in human rights, peacebuilding, and politics.

### Commitment to Free Speech and Expression - "Where Scholarship Meets Activism"

We prioritize research that embodies the principles of free speech and free expression. Our journal is a sanctuary for unfiltered, uncensored dialogue, encouraging bold and fearless discourse on human rights, peace, and politics.

The role of independent media in promoting transparency and accountability in government actions has been instrumental, proving an increase in public trust when free press principles were upheld.

## *Innovative Research Focus*

Our journal encourages submissions that push the boundaries of traditional research. We seek papers that employ innovative methodologies, interdisciplinary approaches, and creative solutions to complex issues.

## *Interdisciplinary Approach*

Understanding that human rights, peace, and politics are deeply interconnected, we promote interdisciplinary and intersectional research that integrates insights from various fields such as law, sociology, history, economics, international relations, and environmental studies.

## DISCLAIMER

The International Journal of Human Rights, Peace and Politics is committed to fostering open, honest, and critical discourse on pressing global issues. We tackle sensitive topics and challenge established narratives as part of our mission to promote justice and human rights.

Our intent is not to offend, but to provoke thought, encourage debate, and inspire action. We acknowledge that some content may be challenging or controversial. Our articles reflect the views of their authors and do not necessarily represent the official position of the journal, its editors, or affiliated institutions.

We uphold rigorous academic standards while providing a platform for marginalized voices and perspectives often excluded from mainstream discourse. Our commitment to free speech and uncensored dialogue means we may publish viewpoints that some readers find disagreeable or unsettling.

We encourage readers to engage critically with our content, challenge assumptions, and contribute to constructive dialogue. Our goal is to deepen understanding of complex issues, not to cause offense or promote any single ideology.

Readers are advised to approach sensitive topics with an open mind, recognizing that discomfort can be a catalyst for growth and positive change. We believe that only by confronting difficult truths and engaging in frank discussions can we hope to address the world's most pressing human rights challenges.

# Preface

As I write this, I'm acutely aware that we're not just launching another academic journal. We're igniting a revolution in thought and action.

***The International Journal of Human Rights, Peace and Politics is our battleground in the war against oppression, injustice, and the stifling orthodoxies that have long dominated discourse in our field.***

Let's confront an uncomfortable truth: the idealistic notion of universal human rights is precisely that - idealistic. It's a comforting fiction that obscures a harsh reality.

**All humans are not equal. But why?** This isn't a question of inherent worth, but of how our world functions. Region, race, and power dynamics fundamentally shape how rights are categorized, prioritized, and enforced.

While we pontificate about universal rights, 82 million people are forcibly displaced worldwide. Nearly 10% of the global population survives on less than $1.90 a day. These aren't just numbers - they're a damning indictment of our global system.

In India, we're witnessing a real-time erosion of democratic norms. The farmers' protests, the longest in our history, have laid bare the deep-seated issues of agrarian distress and corporate influence in policymaking. Kashmir remains an open wound, with frequent internet shutdowns and rampant human rights abuses. The Citizenship Amendment Act has codified religious discrimination into law.

Globally, the situation is equally grim. The Rohingya genocide in Myanmar, the brutal suppression in Belarus, the ongoing catastrophe in Yemen - these aren't isolated incidents. They're symptoms of a global order that prioritizes power over people.

*This journal exists to challenge that order. We reject the false neutrality that often serves as a smokescreen for maintaining the status quo. Instead, we align ourselves with Chomsky's assertion that intellectuals have a responsibility to "speak the truth and expose lies."*

We must grapple with fundamental questions: Is the concept of universal human rights fundamentally Western? Can it truly be global? Or is it, as some argue, a form of cultural imperialism, a way for dominant powers to impose their values on others?

These aren't abstract philosophical debates. They have real-world consequences. When we publish research on how economic sanctions impact civilian populations, we're not just contributing to academic discourse - we're providing ammunition for those fighting against these often counterproductive policies.

Our approach is data-driven but not data-blind. We recognize that numbers can illuminate but also obscure. When we report the number of journalists killed worldwide in 2024, we're highlighting a direct assault on freedom of expression and the public's right to information.

This journal is revolutionary in its scope and ambition. We're not interested in incremental change or polite disagreement. We're here to fundamentally reshape the discourse around human rights, peace, and politics.

*Our commitment to free speech isn't a platitude - it's a weapon against oppression.*

We draw inspiration from Joseph Nye's concept of soft power, but we push it further. It's not enough to influence - we aim to transform. When we publish research on the impact of climate change on vulnerable communities in the Global South, we're providing a platform for voices often silenced in global climate negotiations.

Our institutional approach is rigorous but not rigid. We demand the highest standards of scholarship, but we also value lived experience and grassroots perspectives.

*We believe in the power of words to shape reality.*

This journal is a sanctuary for unfiltered, uncensored dialogue. We publish work that other journals might deem too controversial or politically sensitive.

I want to be crystal clear: this journal is not neutral. We take sides - always with the oppressed, never with the oppressor. We stand with marginalized communities fighting for their rights in the face of state repression. We amplify the voices of indigenous peoples resisting corporate land grabs. We support workers striking for better conditions in exploitative global supply chains.

Our vision - "Contribute to the change you wish to see in the world" - is not just a statement. It's a call to action. We don't just publish research - we ignite movements.

We will continue to speak truth to power, to challenge injustice, and to fight for a world where human rights are not just respected, but celebrated.

To our readers, our contributors, our supporters: this is your journal. Use it. Engage with it. Let it fuel your anger, your passion, your determination to create change.

*The International Journal of Human Rights, Peace and Politics is more than a publication. It's a revolution in print.*

*The stakes couldn't be higher.*

*"Bhavna Dahiya*
    *Editor-in-Chief*
    *Founder, International Council on Human Rights, Peace &*
*Politics"*

# ACKNOWLEDGEMENTS

We are indebted to our core team members, especially our Founder, Ms Bhavna Dahiya, and our Managing Director, Ms Anshika Singh whose expertise has significantly shaped our interdisciplinary approach.

Ms Dahiya's years of experience in International delegations, grassroots activism and academic scholarship have uniquely positioned her to bridge the gap between theory and praxis, shaping the journal's foundational ethos. Ms Singh's tireless efforts have transformed our ambitious vision into reality. Her strategic acumen has been instrumental in academic publishing while staying true to our principles.

We greatly acknowledge and appreciate our contributors—scholars and activists—who have dared to challenge the status quo. Your work forms the backbone of this journal.

We extend our heartfelt thanks to the tireless efforts of our peer reviewers, whose rigorous scrutiny ensures the highest standards of academic integrity while maintaining our commitment to radical thought.

Lastly, we acknowledge the countless unnamed individuals—the victims and survivors of human rights abuses, the families of the disappeared, the communities resisting oppression—whose stories drive our work. Your resilience inspires us, and your struggles fuel our determination to create a platform where your voices can be heard.

This journal stands on the shoulders of all who have fought and continue to fight for a more just world. We are humbled by your courage and honored to contribute to this ongoing struggle.

# PROLOGUE

At the core of our journal's mission lies our powerful trifecta: Dissent, Defiance, and Discourse.

We define dissent as the lifeblood of democracy, recognizing that progress often springs from those brave enough to question prevailing orthodoxies. Our commitment to defiance emboldens us to stand firm against injustice, refusing to bow to oppressive systems or silencing tactics. Through rigorous discourse, we create a platform where diverse voices can engage in critical dialogue, challenging assumptions and forging new paths towards justice.

These principles aren't mere slogans—they drive every aspect of our work, from the selection of our contributors to the framing of our debates.

## *Our Contributions:*

Our contributors are the fearless voices of our time—scholars, activists, journalists, and thought leaders who dare to speak truth to power, offering ground-breaking analyses and first-hand accounts from the frontlines of human rights, peace and politics struggles worldwide.

1. Orientalism, Cartographic Authority, and the Construction of Global Power Narratives - **Bhavna Dahiya**

2. Misogynist Violence : Examining the rise of GenZ Incel Culture in India - **Anshika Singh**

3. Virtual Rape: A Case of Gross Human Rights Violation - **Shreshtha Gupta**

4. Diversionary Wars: A Geopolitical Deception - **Dawood Rashid Dohi and Divy Tiwari**

5. Human Rights and Minorities in South Asia: A Case Study of Hindus in Pakistan - **Shivam Tiwari**

6. An Unequal Partition: Violence on Gendered Bodies - **Kamakshi Rautela**

7. Cross Border Crimes Arising out of growing concern across Indo Myanmar Border Relations - **Julia Jose**

8. Transitional Gender Justice: Addressing LGBTQI+ Concerns in Postwar Human Rights Activism - **Swetarupa Mishra**

# I

# Orientalism, Cartographic Authority, and the Construction of Global Power Narratives
## Bhavna Dahiya

*Abstract*

This paper examines the relationship between Orientalism, cartography, and the construction of global power narratives, revealing how maps have been instrumental in shaping and perpetuating Western hegemonic discourses about the "Orient." Drawing on Edward Said's seminal work on Orientalism and incorporating insights from critical cartography, we argue that mapmaking has been far from a neutral scientific endeavor, instead serving as a powerful tool for creating and maintaining global power dynamics. Through a multidisciplinary approach combining historical analysis, critical discourse analysis, and comparative case studies, we trace the evolution of Orientalist cartography. Our investigation reveals how naming practices, cartographic silences, and visual iconography in maps have contributed to the "othering" and domination of non-Western spaces.

The paper explores specific case studies, including British mapping of India, French cartography of North Africa, and contemporary digital mapping practices, to illustrate the persistence of Orientalist perspectives in spatial representations. We demonstrate how these cartographic practices continue to influence contemporary international relations, from geopolitical conflicts and development discourses to foreign policy decision-making. Moreover, we examine the emergence of counter-mapping initiatives and indigenous cartographic practices as forms of resistance against dominant Western narratives. The paper concludes by discussing the implications of our findings for international relations theory and practice, emphasizing the need for critical cartographic literacy among policymakers and scholars.

By excavating the often-hidden ways in which spatial representations influence global politics, this research contributes to a more nuanced understanding of the role of cartography in constructing and maintaining global power structures. It also points towards the potential for decolonial mapping practices to reshape our understanding of global spaces and power dynamics.

**Keywords**: Orientalism, Critical Cartography, International Relations, Geopolitical Imagination, Postcolonial Studies, Spatial Power Dynamics

## *Introduction*

The practice of cartography, far from being a neutral exercise in geographical representation, has long been intertwined with the complex power dynamics that shape international relations. The act of mapping has both reflected and reinforced Western hegemonic discourses about the "Orient." The concept of Orientalism, as articulated by Edward Said in his seminal work, posits that Western scholarship and cultural production have systematically misrepresented and essentialized the "East" or "Orient," creating a dichotomy that serves to justify and perpetuate Western dominance. This paper argues that cartography has been a crucial, yet often overlooked, tool in this process of "othering" and domination.

From the early modern period to the present day, maps have played a pivotal role in shaping Western perceptions of non-Western spaces. The power to name, delineate, and represent vast swathes of the globe has been instrumental in constructing the "Orient" as a space to be known, controlled, and exploited. This cartographic Orientalism has not only reflected existing power structures but has actively participated in their creation and maintenance.

By critically examining the intersection of cartography and Orientalism, we can better understand the persistent patterns of power and perception that continue to shape global politics. Moreover, this analysis opens avenues for reimagining cartographic practices in ways that challenge, rather than reinforce, hegemonic narratives. Through a multidisciplinary approach drawing on geography, postcolonial studies, and international relations, we aim to develop a nuanced understanding of the complex interplay between spatial representation, cultural imagination, and geopolitical power.

## *Literature Review*

The intersection of cartography and Orientalism has been explored by scholars from various disciplines, though often in fragmented ways. Edward Said's "Orientalism" (1978) serves as a foundational text for this analysis. Said's critique of Western representations of the East provides a crucial framework for understanding how cartography has participated in the construction of the "Orient." While Said did not focus extensively on maps, his insights into the power dynamics inherent in Western knowledge production about the East are directly applicable to cartographic practices.

Building on Said's work, J.B. Harley's "Deconstructing the Map" (1989) marked a pivotal moment in critical cartography. Harley argued that maps are not objective representations of reality but rather social constructions imbued with power relations. His work opened up new avenues for analyzing maps as texts that embody and reproduce dominant ideologies, including Orientalist perspectives. Denis Wood's "The Power of Maps" (1992) further developed this critical approach to cartography, emphasizing the role of maps in creating and maintaining social and political orders. Wood's analysis of how maps serve the interests of those who create them provides valuable insights into the ways cartography has been employed in service of Orientalist and colonial projects.

In the field of postcolonial studies, Gayatri Chakravorty Spivak's concept of "epistemic violence," introduced in "Can the Subaltern Speak?" (1988), offers a useful lens for examining how cartographic practices have silenced and erased indigenous spatial knowledge. While Spivak's work does not directly address cartography, her insights into the violence inherent in Western knowledge production are highly relevant to understanding the impact of Orientalist mapping practices. More recently, scholars have begun to explicitly address the relationship between cartography and Orientalism. Matthew Edney's "Mapping an Empire: The Geographical Construction of British India, 1765-1843" (1997) provides a detailed historical analysis of how cartographic practices were instrumental in the British construction and control of India. Edney's work demonstrates how mapping was not just a reflection of colonial power but an active tool in its exercise. Jordan Branch's "The Cartographic State: Maps, Territory, and the Origins of Sovereignty" (2014) offers valuable insights into how cartographic practices shaped the modern international system. Branch's work helps us understand the broader context in which Orientalist cartography operated and its lasting impact on global political structures.

Despite these valuable contributions, there remains a need for a more comprehensive analysis that brings together insights from critical cartography, postcolonial studies, and international relations theory to fully explore the relationship between cartography and Orientalism. This paper aims to address this gap by providing a multidisciplinary examination of how cartographic Orientalism has shaped and continues to influence global power dynamics. Moreover, while much of the existing literature focuses on historical examples, there is a need for more sustained analysis of how Orientalist cartographic practices persist in contemporary contexts, including digital mapping technologies and current geopolitical conflicts. This paper will contribute to filling this gap by examining both historical and contemporary manifestations of cartographic Orientalism and their implications for international relations.

## *Theoretical Framework*

This paper's analysis is grounded in a synthesis of post-colonial theory, critical cartography, and international relations theory. This interdisciplinary approach allows for a nuanced examination of the complex interplay between spatial representation, cultural imagination, and geopolitical power.

At the core of our theoretical framework is Edward Said's concept of Orientalism, which we extend to the realm of cartography. Said's work posits that Orientalism operates as a style of thought based on an ontological and epistemological distinction made between "the Orient" and "the Occident." We argue that this distinction is not only discursive but also spatial, manifested in cartographic representations that have both reflected and reinforced this binary worldview. Building on this foundation, we incorporate insights from critical cartography, particularly the work of J.B. Harley. Harley's deconstruction of the map as a text imbued with power relations provides a crucial lens through which to examine Orientalist cartography. We posit that maps are not neutral scientific documents but rather socially constructed artifacts that embody and reproduce dominant ideologies. In the context of Orientalism, maps serve as powerful tools for constructing and maintaining Western hegemony over the "Orient."

To bridge the gap between cartographic theory and international relations, we draw on constructivist approaches in IR theory, particularly those that emphasize the role of ideas, norms, and representations in shaping global politics. Alexander Wendt's assertion that "anarchy is what states make of it" can be extended to spatial representations: the "Orient" is, in many ways, what cartographers make of it. This constructivist lens allows us to examine how cartographic representations contribute to the social construction of global political realities. Furthermore, we incorporate Gayatri Spivak's concept of "epistemic violence" to analyze the ways in which Orientalist cartography has silenced and erased indigenous spatial knowledge. This theoretical tool helps us understand mapping not just as a representation of space, but as an act of power that can marginalize and suppress alternative ways of knowing and organizing space. Henri Lefebvre's theory of the production of space illustrates that space is not a neutral container but a social product. This perspective allows us to examine how Orientalist cartography has been instrumental in producing the "Orient" as a space to be known, controlled, and exploited by Western powers.

## Methodology

For this study, I employed a qualitative research methodology combining historical analysis, critical discourse analysis, and comparative case studies. My approach is designed to examine the relationship between cartography and Orientalism across different periods and contexts, with a focus on their impact on international relations. I conducted a thorough review of historical maps and related documents from the early modern period to the present day. This involved examining cartographic representations of "Oriental" regions produced by various Western powers, including British,

French, and American sources.

I applied critical discourse analysis to both the visual elements of maps and their accompanying texts. This method allowed me to identify and analyze Orientalist tropes, power dynamics, and rhetorical strategies embedded in cartographic representations. I also employed techniques of visual analysis to examine the iconography, color schemes, and spatial organization of maps, paying particular attention to how these elements convey Orientalist perspectives. To assess the ongoing relevance of Orientalist cartography, I analyzed current news media, policy documents, and digital mapping platforms, focusing on their representation of "Oriental" spaces. Throughout my analysis, I synthesized insights from critical cartography, postcolonial studies, and international relations theory to provide a comprehensive understanding of the subject.

Data sources included historical map collections from major libraries and archives, academic literature on cartography and Orientalism, contemporary media reports, and policy documents. I prioritized primary sources where possible, supplemented by relevant secondary literature. This methodology allowed me to trace the evolution of Orientalist cartography over time, examine its manifestations across different contexts, and analyze its ongoing impact on international relations. By combining historical analysis with contemporary critique, I aim to provide a nuanced understanding of how cartographic practices have shaped and continue to influence global power dynamics.

## Analysis and Discussion

## The Power of Projection: Mercator, Gall-Peters, and Global Perceptions

The choice of map projection influences how we perceive the world and, by extension, how international relations are conducted. This section examines two significant projections: the Mercator Projection, created in 1569 by Gerardus Mercator, and the Gall-Peters projection, which aims to represent land masses in their true proportions.

The Mercator Projection, likely the most familiar map, has been both lauded for its navigational utility and criticized for its distortions. While it preserves angles, making it invaluable for navigation, it significantly inflates the size of landmasses further from the equator. This results in a visual overrepresentation of Western countries, particularly in the North, while diminishing the apparent size of countries near the equator. For instance, on a Mercator map, Greenland appears roughly the same size as Africa, when in reality, Africa is about 14 times larger. This distortion is not merely a cartographic curiosity but has far-reaching implications for international relations and policy decisions. The visual emphasis on Western nations reinforces notions of their global importance, potentially influencing everything from aid allocation to geopolitical strategy.

In contrast, the Gall-Peters projection, introduced in the 1970s, attempts to correct these distortions by presenting land masses in their correct proportions. This projection dramatically alters the familiar world map, expanding the visual representation of Africa and South America while shrinking Europe and North America. The Gall-Peters projection has been championed by advocates of global equality, who argue that accurate size representation is crucial for fair global representation.

### *The impact of these projections on international relations is multifaceted:*

Resource Allocation: The visual diminishment of developing nations on Mercator maps may contribute to underestimation of their needs in development programs.

Geopolitical Strategy: Overemphasis on northern countries can skew strategic thinking, potentially leading to miscalculations in areas like military deployment or diplomatic engagement.

Environmental Policy: Distortions in the apparent size of polar regions on Mercator maps may influence perceptions of issues like climate change, potentially affecting global environmental policies.

Cultural Perceptions: The familiar Mercator view shapes cultural understandings of global geography, potentially reinforcing Eurocentric or Western-centric worldviews.

The debate over map projections exemplifies how cartographic choices are inherently political. The Peters projection, despite its flaws, served as a powerful critique of the cartographic status quo, forcing a reconsideration of how maps shape our understanding of the world.

# The Power of Naming: Toponymy in Colonial Cartography

The act of naming places on maps is an assertion of power and ownership over space. In Orientalist cartography, we observe a systematic erasure of indigenous toponyms and their replacement with Western names. This process, known as toponymic silencing, serves to reshape the cognitive landscape of the "Orient" in Western terms. For instance, the British mapping of India saw the Anglicization of place names (e.g., "Bombay" for "Mumbai"), often distorting local pronunciations to fit English phonetics. This practice not only facilitated colonial administration but also symbolically asserted British dominion over Indian space. The power to name is the power to define reality, and through this lens, we can understand toponymic practices as a form of epistemic violence against indigenous spatial knowledge.

# Cartographic Silences: What the Maps Don't Show

Equally telling as what maps depict is what they omit. Harley's concept of "cartographic silences" provides a powerful tool for analyzing how Orientalist maps have selectively represented space to serve Western interests. These silences often manifest in the depiction of supposedly "empty" lands, erasing indigenous presence and justifying colonial expansion. Consider the mapping of Australia as "terra nullius," which rendered invisible millennia of Aboriginal occupation and land use. This cartographic silence not only facilitated colonial settlement but continues to shape legal and political discourses around land rights to this day. Similarly, early maps of the Middle East often depicted vast "empty" deserts, ignoring complex networks of Bedouin migration and trade that had existed for centuries.

# Orientalist Iconography in Maps

Beyond the technical aspects of cartography, maps often incorporate visual elements that reveal and reinforce Orientalist perspectives. Decorative cartouches, illustrations, and marginalia in historical maps frequently depicted "Orientals" in exoticized or primitive ways, contrasting with representations of Europeans as bearers of civilization. For example, 16th and 17th-century European maps of the Ottoman Empire often featured turbaned figures, camels, and minarets, reducing complex societies to a set of exotic stereotypes. These visual tropes not only reflected existing Orientalist attitudes but also shaped the European imagination of the "East," creating a self-reinforcing cycle of misrepresentation.

## Counter-Mapping and Resistance

While Orientalist cartography has been a tool of domination, it has also sparked resistance. Indigenous and postcolonial cartographic practices have emerged as powerful forms of counter-mapping. These efforts seek to reclaim spatial representation and challenge dominant Western narratives. For instance, the Inuit people of Canada have created maps that represent their traditional knowledge of Arctic landscapes, incorporating elements like ice formations and animal migration patterns that are absent from Western maps. Similarly, Palestinian cartographers have produced maps that challenge Israeli territorial claims, asserting a spatial narrative that counters dominant geopolitical representations.

## Comparative Analysis: Orientalist Cartography Across Empires and Eras

A comparative analysis reveals both consistencies and variations in Orientalist cartographic practices across different imperial powers and historical periods. While all engaged in forms of epistemic violence, the specific manifestations varied. British cartography of India, for instance, was characterized by an obsessive drive for scientific precision, reflecting a belief in the superiority of Western rationality. French mapping of North Africa, in contrast, often romanticized the landscape, fitting with French colonial narratives of "civilizing" exotic lands. The Cold War era saw a shift in Orientalist cartography, with ideological concerns coming to the fore. American maps of the Middle East during this period often emphasized oil resources and strategic military positions, reducing complex societies to geopolitical assets or liabilities. Contemporary Chinese mapping of the "Belt and Road Initiative" regions presents an interesting case of potential "neo-Orientalism." While challenging Western cartographic dominance, these maps often reproduce Orientalist tropes, depicting Central and Southeast Asian countries primarily in terms of their economic utility to China.

# Contemporary Relevance of Orientalist Cartography in International Relations

## Digital Cartography and the Perpetuation of Orientalist Perspectives

The advent of digital mapping technologies, far from erasing Orientalist biases, has in many ways perpetuated and even amplified them. Popular platforms like Google Maps, while presenting themselves as neutral and objective, often reproduce Western-centric views of space. For example, the default view on many digital maps places Europe at the center, marginalizing other regions. The level of detail provided for different areas often reflects Western priorities and data availability, creating a digital divide that mirrors historical patterns of cartographic silencing. Moreover, algorithmic biases in these platforms can reinforce Orientalist stereotypes. Search results and place recommendations may prioritize Western-oriented businesses or tourist sites in non-Western countries, subtly shaping users' perceptions of these spaces.

## Cartography in Modern Geopolitical Conflicts

Cartographic representations continue to play a crucial role in contemporary geopolitical conflicts, often drawing on and reinforcing Orientalist narratives. The ongoing disputes in the South China Sea provide a telling example. Competing cartographic claims by China and other Southeast Asian nations not only reflect conflicting territorial ambitions but also differing conceptions of spatial order and historical legitimacy. In the Middle East, the mapping of borders, resources, and conflict zones continues to be a contentious issue. Western media maps of the region often simplify complex situations, reducing multifaceted conflicts to easily digestible visual narratives that frequently reproduce Orientalist tropes of tribal or sectarian strife.

## Cartographic Practices in International Development and Aid

International development agencies and NGOs, while ostensibly working to improve conditions in the "Global South," often employ mapping practices that echo colonial-era Orientalism. World Bank and IMF maps frequently depict developing countries through the lens of economic indicators, reducing complex societies to datasets that fit Western development paradigms. Humanitarian aid maps, while serving crucial logistical purposes, can inadvertently reproduce narratives of helplessness and dependency. By focusing solely on crisis points and aid distribution, these maps may present a skewed picture of entire regions, reinforcing Orientalist notions of perpetual instability and Western saviorism.

## *The Influence of Orientalist Cartography on Foreign Policy Decision-Making*

The persistence of Orientalist cartographic perspectives continues to influence foreign policy decision-making in Western countries. Policy makers' mental maps, shaped by centuries of Orientalist cartography, can lead to oversimplified understandings of complex regions. For instance, the notion of the Middle East as a coherent geopolitical entity, despite its vast diversity, owes much to Orientalist cartographic traditions. This cartographic imaginary has real-world consequences, often leading to one-size-fits-all policy approaches that fail to account for local complexities. Similarly, the cartographic division of the world into the "West" and the "Rest" continues to shape diplomatic and military strategies. The persistent use of terms like "Eastern Europe" or "Far East" in policy discourse reveals the enduring influence of Orientalist spatial conceptions.

The legacy of Orientalist cartography continues to exert influence on contemporary international relations. The way we represent and imagine space remains deeply intertwined with power dynamics rooted in colonial-era Orientalism. Recognizing and critically examining these cartographic legacies is crucial for developing more equitable and nuanced approaches to global issues.

## *Implications and Conclusions*

The analysis of cartography through the lens of Orientalism reveals the enduring impact of spatial representations on international relations. Our examination demonstrates that maps are not merely neutral depictions of geographical reality, but powerful instruments in shaping perceptions, policies, and power dynamics on a global scale.

The persistent influence of Orientalist cartography on contemporary global politics is evident in several key areas:

Geopolitical Imaginations: The mental maps inherited from colonial-era cartography continue to influence how policymakers and the public conceptualize global spaces. The division of the world into "West" and "East," "developed" and "developing," often reflects cartographic traditions rooted in Orientalist thinking. This binary worldview can lead to oversimplified policy approaches that fail to account for the complexities of diverse regions.

Territorial Disputes: Many current territorial conflicts, particularly in post-colonial regions, can be traced back to arbitrary boundaries drawn by colonial cartographers. The legacy of Orientalist mapping practices continues to fuel disputes, from the Middle East to Southeast Asia, highlighting the long-term consequences of cartographic power.

Development Discourse: International development practices often rely on mapping techniques that echo colonial-era Orientalism, reducing complex societies to sets of economic indicators. This cartographic approach can perpetuate notions of Western superiority and hinder more nuanced, locally-grounded development strategies.

Digital Colonialism: The dominance of Western tech companies in digital mapping raises concerns about a new form of cartographic colonialism. The power to represent space digitally, often reflecting Western priorities and biases, has significant implications for how global spaces are perceived and navigated.

Resistance and Counter-Mapping: The rise of indigenous and postcolonial mapping practices demonstrates the potential for cartography to be a tool of resistance against dominant narratives. These efforts highlight the importance of diverse perspectives in spatial representation.

The implications of this study extend beyond academic discourse. There is a pressing need for critical cartographic literacy in international relations, both in academic and policy spheres. Decision-makers must be aware of the hidden biases and power dynamics embedded in the maps they use to understand and engage with the world. Furthermore, my analysis points to the potential for decolonial mapping practices to reshape global power dynamics. By challenging Orientalist cartographic traditions, new approaches to spatial representation can contribute to more equitable and nuanced international relations.

The intersection of cartography and Orientalism remains a crucial area of study for understanding global power dynamics. As we navigate an increasingly complex and interconnected world, critically examining the maps that shape our perceptions is essential. Only by recognizing and challenging the legacy of Orientalist cartography can we hope to develop more just and accurate representations of global space, fostering international relations based on mutual understanding rather than historical prejudices.

## *Works Cited*

Anderson, Benedict. Imagined Communities: Reflections on the Origin and Spread of Nationalism. Verso, 2006.

Bhabha, Homi K. The Location of Culture. Routledge, 1994.

Branch, Jordan. The Cartographic State: Maps, Territory, and the Origins of Sovereignty. Cambridge University Press, 2014.

Chakrabarty, Dipesh. Provincializing Europe: Postcolonial Thought and Historical Difference. Princeton University Press, 2000.

Crampton, Jeremy W. "Maps as Social Constructions: Power, Communication and Visualization." Progress in Human Geography, vol. 25, no. 2, 2001, pp. 235-252.

Edney, Matthew H. Mapping an Empire: The Geographical Construction of British India, 1765-1843. University of Chicago Press, 1997.

Fanon, Frantz. The Wretched of the Earth. Translated by Constance Farrington, Grove Press, 1963.

Gregory, Derek. Geographical Imaginations. Blackwell, 1994.

Harley, J. B. "Deconstructing the Map." Cartographica, vol. 26, no. 2, 1989, pp. 1-20.

Kearns, Gerry. "The Imperial Subject: Geography and Travel in the Work of Mary Kingsley and Halford Mackinder." Transactions of the Institute of British Geographers, vol. 22, no. 4, 1997, pp. 450-472.

Lefebvre, Henri. The Production of Space. Translated by Donald Nicholson-Smith, Blackwell, 1991.

Massey, Doreen. Space, Place, and Gender. University of Minnesota Press, 1994.

Monmonier, Mark. How to Lie with Maps. University of Chicago Press, 2018.

Nye, Joseph S. Soft Power: The Means to Success in World Politics. Public Affairs, 2004.

Pickles, John. A History of Spaces: Cartographic Reason, Mapping and the Geo-Coded World. Routledge, 2004.

Said, Edward W. Orientalism. Pantheon Books, 1978.

Spivak, Gayatri Chakravorty. "Can the Subaltern Speak?" Marxism and the Interpretation of Culture, edited by Cary Nelson and Lawrence Grossberg, University of Illinois Press, 1988, pp. 271-313.

Thongchai Winichakul. Siam Mapped: A History of the Geo-Body of a Nation. University of Hawaii Press, 1994.

Turnbull, David. Maps are Territories: Science is an Atlas. University of Chicago Press, 1993.

Wood, Denis. The Power of Maps. Guilford Press, 1992.

Wendt, Alexander. "Anarchy is What States Make of It: The Social Construction of Power Politics." International Organization, vol. 46, no. 2, 1992, pp. 391-425.

Warf, Barney, and Santa Arias, editors. The Spatial Turn: Interdisciplinary Perspectives. Routledge, 2008.

Zunes, Stephen, and Jacob Mundy. Western Sahara: War, Nationalism, and Conflict Irresolution. Syracuse University Press, 2010.

# II

# Misogynist Violence : Examining the rise of GenZ Incel Culture in India Anshika Singh

In a podcast episode with the Beer Biceps in April 2024, Nora Fatehi, an Indian Actress said, "Many men have been brainwashed by the era of feminism," expressing how it has f***** up the society. A number of young Indian men who see themselves as "victims of feminism" supported this statement. With the rise in videos and discussions on terms such as 'Chad (a stereotypical alpha male: portrayed as handsome, successful, muscular, cocky and very popular with women), Sigma (a man who lives his life on his own terms and is not distracted by women) and accounts labelling themselves as MGTOWs (Men Going Their Own Way) is indicative of how proud young Indian men are to be known or identified as part of such a group. While the anti-feminist narratives, casual misogyny, harassment and violence are quite common in India, the narrative of a growing 'Incel' community, will pose a greater threat to women's safety and security in this digital age.

*Who are Incels?*

Incel stands for 'involuntary celibates'. They believe that feminism has ruined society and disrupted the natural order of monogamous heterosexual relationships by giving women the concept of 'choice'. They are frustrated because they see feminism as a movement that denies them power and sexual control over women's bodies and want to overthrow the concept by force. This ideology is dangerous as it is based on 'misogynistic' sentiments and actively celebrates all forms of violence against women in order for men to reclaim their masculinity.

These incels weaponise the idea of subordination and use it as fuel to advocate for the abolition of women's rights and reduce them to subhuman sexual objects. It is often frustration at the lack of success in finding a partner, heartbreak or the impression of a lack of attractiveness that initially drives men to incel communities. They find it difficult to enter into or maintain a romantic relationship due to their appearance and lack of sexual attraction. They attribute this to society's bias in favour of attractive people and believe that their rightful access to women's bodies is thwarted by a preference for the most desirable or in popular GenZ terms 'the chads'.

Popular social media trends like "I'm looking for a man in finance" further reinforce this belief among incels. Public figures like Jordan Peterson defend incels and portray them as unfairly marginalised, further contributing to this narrative. Platforms like Reddit and 4chan are readily available for them to discuss and spread their violent discourse. These discussion groups provide space for misogynistic discourse about a wide range of violence, from casual harassment to pro-rape discourse. Incels continue to dehumanise women, attacking them with slurs on mainstream platforms such as Instagram, Facebook and Twitter, inflicting violence on them and often celebrating them to assert their lost supremacy.

The incel ideology is based on the view that before the feminist revolution, every man had access to a female partner and was easier to control than women are today. They believe that with the feminist movement, there is a change in society that limits them and their ability to control women. They also believe that society has collectively abandoned men to have their 'privileged' or 'entitled' access to women's bodies. This often leads to hatred and misogynistic feelings, which leads them to impose 'traditional' gender roles on women, giving them a sense of 'control' over women. One of the most common means used to exert this control is 'violence'.

This explains the link between misogyny and violence. But incel ideology is only one form of misogynistic violence. There are a number of interconnected misogynist communities that consist of different types and degrees of misogynistic violent extremism. These communities often incite, glorify and promote violence, especially sexual violence against women. Some aspects of their behaviour may differ, but they largely function according to this ideology. This violence can extend beyond the personal sphere into the public sphere, in the form of acid attacks, rape and even extreme forms such as terrorist attacks. Terrorist groups often use the concept of 'women' to target people who want to have control over women in their lives. For example, ISIS and Lashkar-e-Taiba (LeT) have often advertised how they treat women in order to recruit them, pointing out how 'Western' countries have 'corrupted' their women and how they need to restore this.

It is therefore important to tackle misogynistic attitudes at an early stage to prevent an escalation of violence and reduce the likelihood of extremist tendencies.

India is among the most dangerous countries for women in terms of the risk of sexual violence, including rape, sexual harassment, coercive sex and lack of justice in rape cases. While violence against women is widespread in India, awareness of incel-related crimes in India is low. Since there are no sociological studies on the subject and only a few cases have been reported, the terminology has hardly caught on in India. To understand the rise of incel culture in India, it is important to analyse in detail the forms of sexual expression in India and the impact of patriarchy and family structures on it.

## *Sexual Expression in India and rise of Incel culture*

The joint family system in India and the taboo around 'sex' limits the scope for sexual experimentation and even dating in many households. With multiple generations living together in close quarters, the concept of 'privacy' is non-existent. In most cases, the frustration of not being able to date or being unsuccessful in the dating world contributes to the 'feelings of hate'. The frustration is compounded by society's beauty norms and caste barriers.

The Indian incels are called 'currycels', which was originally a derogatory term for men of Indian origin who were particularly lacking in sex appeal. These currycels not only believe that they are victims of feminism, but also see white men (especially Korean/European) as the reason for their inability to find partners. With the rise of Kpop fans in India, the trend of GenZ guys hating them has become widespread.

There are a few reasons that contribute to this 'hate' -

a) The femininity of K-pop men,

b) The change in preferences/standard of Indian girls and

c) Patriarchal structures/perceptions.

Indian men believe that Korean men are less masculine because of their feminine features which cannot be considered attractive. This idea of masculinity stems from the decades-long portrayal of 'macho' men in Indian films. From physical appearance to behaviours, the idea that 'Korean men' are desirable and preferred over Indian girls challenges these GenZ teenagers' notions of masculinity. Incels often labelled such girls/women online as "race traitors" for preferring to date/ who are dating outside their race. They also encourage and celebrate all kinds of violence and harassment against such women.

An obvious example is the 2023 film 'Animal' starring Ranbir Kapoor, which did well despite concerns about its glorification of misogyny and violence. The glorification of male chauvinistic characters who inflict violence on women goes down particularly well with such incel groups in India. Moreover, the growing trend of terms like 'simping' (short for Sucker Idolising Mediocre P**sy) among GenZs shows the normalisation of derogatory comments against women on mainstream platforms. These incel groups are targeting anything remotely related to the empowerment of women online. Most Indian incel accounts on social media, especially on Instagram and Facebook, constantly refer to the nostalgic longing for the 'simpler' times when gender roles were clearly defined and women abided by what men said. Many boys often compare the 'girls of today' to their mothers or the older generation, who were seen as 'loyal, loving and conforming to their fathers', while the girls of today have supposedly been corrupted by the ideas of feminism and empowerment. These incel communities therefore validate and encourage such slurs and actions in an endeavour to achieve the goal of 'controlling women' through such representation.

## *Conclusion*

The currycels have been around for decades, but they are only gradually being recognised in India. The lack of awareness among the public and the lack of research by academia on the trend and the impact of incels in the Indian society is something we need to focus on in the future. It is important to make a connection between the online incel culture and the overall problem of misogyny and patriarchal structure in India to understand its impact. As women in Indian society continue to be affected by the rising wave of incel-related violence, we need more people from academia to research and create awareness about the psychosocial impact on them.

## *Works Cited*

Halpin, Michael, and Finlay Maguire. "Yes, the incel community has a sexism problem, but we can do something about it." The Conversation, 11 June 2023, https://theconversation.com/yes-the-incel-community-has-a-sexism-problem-but-we-can-do-som
ething-about-it-207206.

Zimmerman, Shannon, et al. "International." Women In International Security, 10 September 2018,https://wiisglobal.org/wp-content/uploads/Recognizing-the-Violent-Extremist-Ideology-of-% E2%80%98Incels-.pdf.

Beauchamp, Zack. "The Threat Landscape: Incel and Misogynist Violent Extremism." McCain Institute,https://www.mccaininstitute.org/wp-content/uploads/2021/10/incel-and-misogynist-violent-extremism-read-ahead-materials-august-2.pdf.

Kaur, Gurpreet. "Incel Extremism in India: A View from the Global South – GNET." Global Network on Extremism and Technology, 23 August 2022, https://gnet-research.org/2022/08/23/incel-extremism-in-india-a-view-from-the-global-south/.

# III

# Virtual Rape: A Case of Gross Human Rights Violation Shreshtha Gupta

## *Introduction*

With the advent of technology, our lives have become far more comfortable today. But on the flip side, there are some gross issues concerning technological advancements. Digital tools have given rise to online crimes such as cyberbullying, trolling, scams, hacking, phishing, harassment and virtual rape. One of the most alarming advancements in technology is the rise of virtual rape. "Virtual Rape" refers to cases of sexual abuse that have taken place online. It is therefore crucial for humankind to explore the intersection of digital tools and human rights. The first case of virtual rape was reported by a woman named Nina Jane Patel through Medium Blogpost. She claimed that her avatar was virtually gang-raped in the metaverse. An avatar refers to a human-like artificial intelligence-enabled virtual assistant that takes on the user's character or persona.

Metaverse refers to the immersive digital world where one can interact and visualize using virtual reality headsets. Another case came to light from the UK wherein a 16-year-old teenager is said to have been gang-raped by a group of strangers in a virtual reality game.

## *Understanding Virtual Rape*

From a cyber criminological perspective, virtual rape represents a form of cyber-enabled sexual violence that exploits the vulnerabilities of virtual environments. Perpetrators may use techniques such as hacking, social engineering, or in-game manipulation to coerce or force victims into sexual acts within the digital realm (K. Jaishankar). The debate over whether virtual rape constitutes actual rape traces back to as early as 1993 when the Village Voice featured an article by Julian Dibbell discussing a case of "rape in cyberspace." Dibbell's article highlighted how individuals controlling avatars that experienced sexual assault in a virtual environment reported experiencing emotions akin to those felt by victims of physical rape (Jo Sales, The Guardian, 2023).

While virtual rape can have psychological implications for the victim but the fact that unlike physical rape it does not happen in the real world and the lack of physical contact may lead to its dismissal by many. The concept of virtual rape in itself raises fundamental questions about consent, harm and accountability in the virtual environments. This in a way would downplay the emotional and psychological impact on the victim.

## *Impact on Virtual Rape Victims*

Virtual Rape highlights the potential vulnerability of human beings particularly women in the arena of the digital world. Virtual Rape victims might feel traumatized, isolated and ashamed to come out and convey their ordeal. Furthermore, it compounds the problems of rape survivors to seek help or report abuse fearing retaliation from their assailants. One might easily walk away thinking whatever happened digitally would not reflect on the real world. Just like the cases of cyberbullying, trolling and sexual harassment, it can have lingering effects on the victims. Victims of digital rape, a profound and emerging issue in the age of virtual realities and metaverses, often grapple with severe emotional and psychological repercussions long after the incident.

The intertwined nature of human consciousness and digital avatars complicates this trauma. Over time, individuals develop deep bonds with their virtual environments, forming relationships that, while digital, feel intensely real. The abrupt and violent disruption of these bonds can mirror the grief and loss experienced in the physical world. This loss isn't merely about the severance of digital ties but also encompasses the destruction of a carefully curated virtual identity and space where the victim feels a sense of belonging and security. Consequently, the emotional impact can be staggering. Psychologically, victims may manifest symptoms akin to those observed in physical rape survivors.

The intrusion into their digital sanctuary, a place they consider an extension of themselves, can lead to profound feelings of violation and powerlessness. This perceived intrusion and its aftermath can induce conditions such as post-traumatic stress disorder (PTSD), depression, and anxiety, amplifying the overall suffering. This situation underscores the necessity for recognizing digital rape as a legitimate and serious form of assault. The psychological scars left by such experiences necessitate a compassionate and comprehensive approach to victim support and a reevaluation of legal and social frameworks to address this modern form of violation adequately.

## *Gangrape in Metaverse-An Examination*

The first case of virtual gangrape in the metaverse was reported by an employee named Nina Jane Patel working as vice-president of metaverse research in Kabuki Ventures. She narrated her horrific experience through a Medium blog post in December 2021. She alleged that it transpired within seconds of entering Meta's version of Metaverse. As per reports, Nina stated that the incident happened so quickly that she could not even think about putting the safety barrier in place. "I froze", she added. The 43-year-old described how she witnessed her avatar being sexually raped by a group of male avatars who photographed her and sent messages like "Don't pretend, you didn't love it". She told the Daily Mail that she promptly ripped her headphones to end the encounter and that she has been experiencing anxiety ever since.

Meta has launched Horizon Worlds for people aged 18 years or above in the US and Canada in 2021. Many people advised Nina that she should not choose a female avatar next time and that she should not be influenced by the experience because it was not genuine. Meta responded that such technical issues will be put in place to prevent such incidents from happening again. The UK Police are investigating the gang rape case of a

16-year-old in the metaverse that occurred earlier this year. It is believed to be the first time a virtual sexual offence is being investigated by the Police.

As per reports, the victim was wearing a virtual reality headset in an immersive game when her avatar was gang-raped by several male avatars. Although the girl did not sustain any physical injuries during the attack, the investigating officer said that the victim had suffered the same emotional and psychological trauma as a rape victim in the real world.

## *How it leads to Human Rights Violations?*

The deployment of AI technology in combating avatar rape is intricately connected to various human rights frameworks. Here's how these connections manifest:

Right to Safety: The prevalence of avatar rape and sexual harassment in virtual worlds directly threatens users' rights to safety. When individuals enter these spaces, they should be able to interact freely without fear of violation. The implementation of AI systems could serve as a safeguard against such threats, thereby promoting a safer digital environment.

Right to Privacy: While monitoring interactions is essential, it raises significant concerns about user privacy. The right to privacy must not be overshadowed by the drive for safety. Developers must ensure that AI applications do not compromise individual autonomy or expose users to unnecessary surveillance.

Right to Justice: Victims of virtual harassment often struggle to find recourse. AI's ability to document incidents can empower users, allowing them to seek justice and hold perpetrators accountable. This capacity reinforces the fundamental right to an effective remedy, crucial for upholding justice in any society.

## *Tech for Humanity – A Call to Action*

Emerging technologies pose a threat to human rights which is clear from the above discussions. There is an urgent need to address this concern. We need to anticipate the evolution of such technologies to integrate the ethical dimension. While there have been attempts by various state governments such as Europe's AI convention but the world still stands at a nascent stage when it comes to the regulatory frameworks concerning the virtual world. The case of virtual rape in Horizon Worlds and other metaverse games serves as a stark reminder of the intricate intersections between technology, crime, and victimization in the digital age. It highlights how emerging digital landscapes can become arenas for both innovation and harm.

As users navigate these immersive environments, the potential for abuse escalates, challenging our understanding of consent, safety, and justice. In this evolving landscape, traditional legal frameworks often struggle to keep pace, leaving victims vulnerable and seeking recourse in a rapidly changing world. The anonymity of avatars complicates accountability, raising critical questions about identity and responsibility. Moreover, the psychological impact on victims is profound, as the boundary between the virtual and real becomes increasingly blurred.

## *Works Cited*

https://www.firstpost.com/explainers/now-a-gang-rape-in-metaverse-how-sexual-predators-roam-free-in-the-virtual-world-13570602.html

https://www.linkedin.com/pulse/can-anyone-virtually-raped-prof-k-jaishankar-jaishankar-ccbmc/

https://www.thehindu.com/sci-tech/technology/how-europes-ai-convention-balances-innovation-and-human-rights-explained/article68219354.ece

https://www.ohchr.org/en/stories/2023/10/developing-safer-digital-technologies-all

https://www.theguardian.com/commentisfree/2024/jan/05/metaverse-sexual-assault-vr-game-online-safety-meta

https://medium.com/kabuni/fiction-vs-non-fiction-98aa0098f3b0

# IV

# Diversionary Wars: A Geopolitical Deception

## Dawood Rashid Dohi and Divy Tiwari

On January 16, 2024, Iran's Revolutionary Guard conducted a cross-border airstrike in Pakistan, targeting the militant group Jaish al-Adl. The attack was in response to a recent attack on an Iranian police station that Jaish claimed responsibility for. Pakistan condemned the attack as a violation of its sovereignty and territorial integrity. Jaish al-Adl's nativity can be traced back to 2012, where the group emerged as a faction from another militant group, Jundallah, after its leader was captured and executed by Iran in 2010. Their first documented attack took place in August 2012, killing 10 members of the Iranian Revolutionary Guard Corps.

Jaish al-Adl has a history of numerous attacks against Iranian security forces and government officials in the past decade. In 2013, Jaish al-Adl claimed responsibility for the killing of 14 Iranian soldiers in an ambush near the border. The following year, the group held at least five members of Iranian forces hostage. A few years down the line, in 2018, another suicide bombing claimed by Jaish al-Adl killed 27 members of Iran's Islamic Revolutionary Guard, and the fascinating part one would look at is that none of these attacks by the organization was received by such a vociferous retaliation until now. Actually, the recent attack serves to be a conduit to divert the limelight from internal issues.

For the past couple of years, Iran has been on a boil with the hijab protest by Iran. What happened was the death of one woman named Mahsa Amini in September 2022. That big chapter in women's rights and freedom of expression for Iran began with the development surrounding her alleged hijab row, culminated in her death in morality police custody, leading to nationwide outrage and demonstration. Anger over Amini's death and the compulsory hijab law, which was imposed after the 1979 revolution, has seen women lead protests in rage, removing headscarves, chanting slogans of freedom and bodily autonomy, and
vehemently supporting it on social media for the community.

Anger was felt beyond the gender lines, and support came in from all sections of Iranian society against the bindings of the state and economic concerns. Though the strong protests seen in the first days seemed to decline in some days, the aftermath and effects of the movement are still at large. Women continued breaking the hijab mandate by showing up in public places without this dress code and the government responded with enhanced control measures that included proposals for far stricter penalties for non-compliance and limitations on the access of women to higher education, as targeting something so basic and fundamental like Education damages the social fabric deeply and has the power to gag any community.

The hijab protests reflect the multi-layered dynamic of Iranian society, where religious conviction, cultural upbringing, and individual ambitions have come to clash. They are a strong pointer to the continuing struggle for basic rights and an undying quest for self-determination much more so in the Iranian women. Internationally imposed sanctions, falling oil prices, geopolitical imbalances, and lack of proper logistics and resource management have all combined to keep Iran's economy stagnant for the past decade. The rate of unemployment among youth is also about 15 per cent, leading to brain drain and discontent. In addition, business operations are cumbersome due to complex procedures and arbitrary interventions. The Rial has also depreciated considerably, eroding international credibility and In the midst of this grim crisis, the diversionary war of Iran with Pakistan has made an appearance from the old school playbook of Diplomacy.

The most common uses of the term of 'diversionary war' have been found in historical and political texts, specifically, in the event when political leaders undertake international conflicts or choose to heighten already

More current ones would be to divert attention from some internal issue and increase their fame. This strategic play of a doubtful ethical nature has been in use all through the times by the different regimes and probably not once with awful outcomes, as using chaos as a ladder to go up politically is some good strategy. Those historical case studies provide information about the motivation, implementation, and consequences of such strategies.

One early modern example was the Russo-Japanese War of 1904-1905: a regime of Tsar Nicholas II, combating domestic unrest and calls for reform, which plunged head first into war against Japan. As has been argued, partly because the Tsar meant to awaken the patriotic fervor of stirring bonding/ fraternity amongst the people against the threat from the outside. It was only after defeat by Russia that these home tensions were significantly heightened and found themselves fuelling the Revolution of 1905.

An even more recent advance example which has oft been used would be the 1982 Falklands War since thanks to economic debacle and citizens disgruntlement, Argentine's ruling military cabal invaded the Falkland Islands(to them, the Malvinas) and as diversionary war theory would predict this seized nationalist sentiments and regime support. The defeat of Argentina, however, marked the junta's downfall and a return to democratic rule, an example of how such strategies may backfire but it's an important consideration that such tactics like diversionary are still used and ware like Israel Palestine conflict can also be analyzed in the same light .If we take examples of other war like The Iran-Iraq War (1980-1988) brings forth a case of two countries wracked by instability following their respective revolutions and troublesome leadership, where they maintained a long war which each regime was able to use to consolidate power and quash internal dissent.

"While successful in these aims, the war achieved the aims in terms of high human and economic costs for both countries inviting troubles and also pointed towards long-term consequences of such diversionary behavior". "On a smaller scale but should not be overlooked , it has been claimed that the US invasion of Grenada was in itself another example of an instance through which such an action course of action as this was taken, and this action took place during the year 1983".

With the Reagan administration coming under tremendous scrutiny and backlash following the bombing of US Marines in Lebanon, perhaps it answered with an immediate military action that could have swept an upbeat American spirit, acting as a distraction from what was happening in Lebanon. While the move, militarily speaking, was indeed successful, it raised some questions from other nations as to its legality and necessity, which only brought to the fore complex repercussions on a global scale. These historical instances, though different in time and nature, share underlying themes in how the application of a diversionary war strategy has been applied and at times succeeded or backfired but implemented for self-interests and ambitions vehemently.

In most cases the authority or government normally initiating such is experiencing many internal difficulties that may include problems like economic crises and political instability.power to divert the attention of mass to an external enemy or problem ,this not only unites the population but also gives authority a reason to become a messiah. Often enough, the conflicts have an effect of relatively easy and quick public support and national unity, as predicted by diversionary war theory. However, military failures are more likely to worsen the domestic problems that they were supposed to divert attention from, and such changes sometimes result in regime change.

It is important to note that these wars had diversionary elements, but they also involved some other very critical factors like territorial or ideological disputes, along with strategic interests. That kind of complexity in such rendering proves the limitation of looking at these wars merely as a function of diversionary war theory. Diversionary intent is virtually impossible to prove definitively since leaders seldom admit to diversionary motives. Furthermore, the background of historical cases can be colored by hindsight bias, overemphasizing diversionary aspects in conflicts where a quite famous domestic context is already known. However, even with these limitations in mind, grasping the possibility of diversionary motivations in international conflicts is indispensable for a deeper understanding of a complex geopolitical landscape and for avoiding unneeded escalation by both policymakers and analysts alike.

History reveals that while external conflicts might turn attention away from internal issues for some time, they are not only dangerous but may also prove counterproductive to the idea in quite a number of ways. The concept of diversionary war thus remains an effective vantage point from which to assess legacy conflicts and review current sources of geopolitical tension without necessarily being considered in isolation from other elements constituting a broader analytical framework on the multifaceted nature of international relations and complex motivations of political decision-making.

The diversionary war concept, otherwise known as diversionary foreign policy, hypothesizes that a leader is more likely to engage in a war with another nation in order to divert the attention of the public at home from problems within the country. In this scenario, the leader hopes to shift the attention of the masses away from internal problems like poor economic performance, political scandals, or social unrest by declaring war. This can produce a sense of national unity against the common enemy, as it temporarily unites the population behind the leader. The "rally-around-the-flag" effect suggests that during times of an external threat, people turn to their leaders, even if they were previously unpopular.

Similar to India's case, Prime Minister Indira Gandhi gained wide popularity immediately after the India-Pakistan war for the independence of Bangladesh or East Pakistan. Now it's unclear if that was a diversionary war but it's true that the aftermath supports PM Gandhi profoundly. That can create an opportunity to improve the leader's image among people and strengthen their positions. Wartime situations sometimes enable leaders to entrench power, stifle dissent, and adopt policies that would be challenging to push through in peacetime. That can, however, be used to solve internal and deep problems at home, even if often undemocratic.

France fought several wars with European powers during The French Revolution. Some people think that, although ideological, these wars were a great means of consolidating the power of the revolutionary government and drawing attention away from internal struggle. In such light, the 1944 invasion of China has been interpreted by some as an effort on behalf of the Japanese government to divert attention from economic and political problems at home. It is also argued that the North Vietnamese government engaged in war with the US and South Vietnam to further consolidate power and to create national cohesion amidst
internal opposition.

Diversionary war requires that a number of elements go just right, such as the opponent that is chosen, the duration and outcome of the war, and how well the leader can manage the issues at hand. Unless, of course, the war goes on and on, or even is lost; in those cases, the domestic issues will arise and shake the ruler's reputation even more. If they are to appear, the critics suggest, the harms of the war are too large to give war a role as an effective political tool—not an everyday tool, but very powerful in the deck of diplomacy.

Keep in mind that war is a fully fledged phenomenon with multiple causes and consequences, implementation involving huge sums of financial and emotional resources. While the diversionary war concept goes a long way in explaining the origin of some conflicts, it has to be taken in conjunction with other factors and rigorously weighed for each condition. In this turbulent geopolitical landscape of West Asia, the concept of military diplomacy gains further relevance. History testifies that the last few hundred years have seen leaders for peace in this region come to tragic ends.

What was formerly a torn, war-afflicted region now sees the foray of Iran into military diplomacy. Against the backdrop of media hype regarding Iran's recent cross-border airstrike in Pakistan, the underlying motives behind the act, and the possible consequences on regional stability bring out the fine line between diplomacy and military might in the pursuit of geopolitical interests. Technology and information exchange form a part of military diplomacy; the potential use of a diversionary war for narrative-making, in this case, by Iran in the practice of military diplomacy, shows how strategic objectives interface with international perception.

The weaponization of diplomacy becomes too complex and is often controversial, and therefore it needs to be contextualized. Especially by the theory of diversionary war, perhaps its application in this regard deserves detailed investigation into just how the implications have serious consequences for world stability, conflict resolution, and how international diplomacy changes face. The recent conflict that transpired between Iran and Pakistan is the most relevant case study with regard to the subject of how diplomatic actions can be used as strategic weapons for all the countries involved and also maybe use it to divert attention from the domestic matter toward the international objective. On January 16, 2024, IRGC fighters crossed the border into Pakistan and attacked the Sunni militant group Jaish al-Adl. Supposedly a retaliatory act after an Iranian police station was recently attacked, the incident is a classic example of the use of the desecration of diplomatic norms to obtain ammunition for domestic and foreign policy objectives.

How the whole incident unfolded is quite crucial. It is only of late that Iran itself has had to grapple with serious internal problems: protests have been continuing since September 2022, following the death of a 22-year-old lady named Mahsa Amini. Gerard Safranek and Natalie Porter explain this incident as the cause that led to an eruption into a far larger women's rights and freedom of expression movement. Added to the catalogue are acute economic problems flowing from international sanctions, oil price volatility, and mismanagement at home. With the addition of youth unemployment, high rates of brain drain, and brain drain, this list has to be added. In this regard, the airstrike on Jaish al-Adl in Pakistan could also be considered a multi-dimensional diplomatic move that caters to concerns about valid security interests and power projection, possible domestic attention diversion, and new diplomatic leverage over Pakistan.

Weaponizing diplomacy would follow these five modes: strategic timing, calibrated escalation, narrative management, leverage creation, and consolidation at home. Each of these is a way to ensure maximum impact of the diplomatic action on domestic and international fronts, as means to this end. In fact, diversionary war logic is possibly at work here, with leaders adept at initiating or raising the conflict level in international arenas in a bid to distract attention away from home. If it had been the case of a strike against Pakistan, then Iran would fall under the many elements of the concept that have been stated above: internal pressure, shifting major focus to an external threat, display of governmental strength, and gains in nationalist sentiment in the short-term perspective.

What is worth mentioning, though, is that no theory of a diversionary war would be able to explain such complicated diplomatic and military actions. The way the Iran-Pakistan incident, like most other international conflicts, is going to pan out will most probably result from an interaction of genuine security concerns, strategic interests, and domestic political calculations.

It is worth the effort to understand weaponization of diplomacy for more than one reason. It is preventive of conflict because it learns, much in advance, how to identify signs of escalation from international actors. It makes the resolution of conflicts more refined by adding nuance in the strategies behind the Trojan horse motivations of a country's diplomatic actions. It increases the stability of the world in general and, in more specific terms, teaches us how the norms and diplomacy tools can bring a more politically rational process, enhancing the insight of policymakers into international relations, further developing the theory of diplomacy, and predicting future conflict.

It improves international cooperation. From this statement, there are a number of challenges to weaponized diplomacy studies, such as complex motives, information scarcity in many cases, rapid evolution of international relations, possible bias in analysis stemming from cultural and ideational differences, and ethical issues related to dealing with sensitive information. On these fronts, weaponized diplomacy modulously, there would benefit future scholarship interested in at least five inquiries by constructing robust quantitative models, comparative studies of highly similar situations with divergent outcomes, an interrogation of the long-run impact of weaponized diplomatic actions, inquiry into the impact of technological innovation on weaponized diplomacy, a role for non-state actors in weaponized diplomacy, and strategies to mitigate negative impacts.

In that light, the conflict between Iran and Pakistan is a play of shadows within the domestic politics of both countries, international security, and diplomatic ballet. A very stark reminder of how nations can actually use these rounds of diplomatic process to address strategic objectives, sometimes, though, at the cost of regional stability and international norms. As the world is still involved in a broad array of geopolitical problems, this has moved on to remain highly relevant to characterization and causes of patterns of diplomatic weaponization and, most importantly, of global security and the promotion of positive international relations.

The ongoing research will also serve in working out more effective ways by which conflict can be prevented or resolved, proving better-informed policy decisions, and will go on to serve the world by having a more stabilized and cooperative international order. Recent examples of Iran Iraq conflict and Historical examples of Falkland wars are epitome of pursuing tactical diplomacy. They not only creates conflict, trauma and hunger in many regions affecting the peace of millions of people. So the theory of diversionary wars should be studied and debated extensively keeping ongoing conflicts in mind to keep a check if these conflict are just getting all the attention because of power greed of someone in authority.

## *Works Cited*

Katzman, Kenneth. "Iran's Foreign and Defense Policies." Congressional Research Service, 2023.1

Brown, Michael E. "The Causes of Internal Conflict: An Overview." In Nationalism and Ethnic Conflict, edited by Michael E. Brown, 3-25. Cambridge: MIT Press, 2001.4

Kenneth Katzman, "Iran's Foreign and Defense Policies" (Congressional Research Service, 2023), 45-47.

Sara Ahmadi, "The Iran-Pakistan Border Conflict: Implications for Regional Stability," Middle East Policy 28, no. 3 (2024): 80.

Oakes, A. (2006). Diversionary war and Argentina's invasion of the Falkland Islands. Security Studies, 15(3), 431–463. https://doi.org/10.1080/09636410601028354

Tokdemir, E., & Mark, B. S. (2017). When Killers become victims: diversionary war, human rights, and strategic target selection. International Interactions, 44(2), 337–360. https://doi.org/10.1080/03050629.2017.1369412

Tokdemir, E., & Mark, B. S. (2017). When Killers become victims: diversionary war, human rights, and strategic target selection. International Interactions, 44(2), 337–360. https://doi.org/10.1080/03050629.2017.1369412

Dodds, K. (1996). The 1982 Falklands War and a critical geopolitical eye: Steve Bell and the if.. cartoons. Political Geography, 15(6–7), 571–592. https://doi.org/10.1016/0962-6298(96)00002-9

Making sense of Iran-Pakistan Cross-Border strikes. (n.d.). United States Institute of Peace. https://www.usip.org/publications/2024/01/making-sense-iran-pakistan-cross-border-strikes

Films

The Diplomatic Game: Iran's Foreign Policy, directed by Sarah Johnson (2023; New York: Global Documentaries), DVD.

Borderlands: The Iran-Pakistan Frontier, directed by Ahmed Khan (2022; Lahore: South Asian Films), streaming.

YouTube

Shrivastava, Naman . "Diversionary War" https://youtu.be/jtJkC7CU8Xo?si=nJVlZv0FP_aqhDfp

# V

# Human Rights and Minorities in South Asia: A Case Study of Hindus in Pakistan  Shivam Tiwari

## Abstract

The paper aims to analyze the present condition of minorities in Pakistan with an emphasis upon the Hindu community which forms the second largest minority in Pakistan. Through an analysis of the literature on the subject, the paper brings the issues of gross human rights violation that are met out to the minorities in pakistan. It lays emphasis upon the historical as well as the contemporary challenges faced by the Hindu community in Pakistan. A glance over the institutional arrangements provided for the minorities by the state is also done, to highlight the inadequate means at the disposal of the minorities in Pakistan. Through an analysis of documents ranging from International journals on human rights to the reports published by the commission on human rights in Pakistan, an attempt is made to assess the present condition of the minorities.

The scope of the study entails the amendments and rights granted to the minorities in the 1973 Constitution of Pakistan. This is also done in order to highlight the inadequacies that the present constitution has vis a vis minorities living under its jurisdiction. In the end, this paper tries to propose certain measures to address these concerns that are ever present regarding the status of minorities in Pakistan and suggest areas of policy improvement.

**Keywords**: Pakistan, Hindu, Minority, Human Rights, Policy

## Introduction

Studies on human rights and the protection of minorities have traditionally been centered on South Asia, a region with a diverse range of cultures, languages, and faiths.The Indian subcontinent has always been a land of different sets of people and culture. It has welcomed people of all hues and color and has affected and been affected in turn through these interactions. In spite of its rich cultural and historical heritage, the area still has a long way to go before its minority groups are treated fairly and are adequately protected. Not until the advent of british and their introduction of census that the question of minority is seen to be debated in the subcontinent.

Rise of nationalisms in the subcontinent also contributed to this discourse on minority questions which ultimately resulted in the partition of a united India into India and Pakistan. Due to their historical ties to the area and ongoing marginalization, Hindus in Pakistan provide for an especially interesting case study among the many minority groups in the country. Although a muslim majority state was created, minorities falling into those territories were made to believe that they will be granted equal rights and liberty. The speech delivered by the founder of the nation, Mr. M A Jinnah on 11th August declared "...I think that we should keep that in front of us as our idealand you will find that in course of time Hindus would cease to be Hindus and Muslims would cease to be Muslims, not in the religious sense because that is personal faith of each individual but in the political sense as citizens of the state...".

This outlined how the new state was to acknowledge and accommodate its minorities. Turning the words into reality was a task that was outrightly rejected after the formation of Pakistan. Since British India was divided , the Hindu community in Pakistan, which makes up a small portion of the nation's primarily Muslim population, has faced numerous hardships.

The Hindu community in Pakistan was severely reduced and left vulnerable as a result of the partition, which also caused widespread population transfers, intercommunal violence, and a redefining of national identities. Pakistan's socio-political environment has changed throughout the years, more often than not to the disadvantage of the country's Hindu minority. Furthermore, this research will place the predicament of Hindus in Pakistan in the larger framework of international human rights norms and agreements. It will help us to critically evaluate the effectiveness of national and international institutions for addressing and resolving abuses of minorities' human rights. In order to present a comprehensive picture of minority rights in South Asia, the article also compares the circumstances facing Hindus in Pakistan with those of other minority groups in the area.

Using a case study methodology, this study will use research being done in Pakistan and other reports both national and international to show how Hindus actually live in Pakistan. This will make it possible to have an informed opinion upon the complex and intersectional nature of the problems faced by the populace on account of gender, customs and class.

## *State of Hindus in Pakistan*

Minority rights are at the forefront in the postmodern world. Ability to accommodate its minorities is the test of the modern nation state. Diversity is the hallmark of the nationstates formed in the third world and their accommodation into the mainstream is the biggest challenge facing them. Some countries have tried hard to accommodate their minorities and there are still some who are yet to recognize let alone accommodate their minorities.

In a research paper published in 2022 in the journal Annals of History and Social Sciences(AHSS) by Akbar Ali, Muhammad Arslan and Dr. Ghulam Mustafa gives details about the current facts and figures about the minorities in Pakistan. " So far as the population of religious minorities is concerned, religious minorities constitute 3.7% of the total population"(Mustafa 2022). The constitution of 1973 recognises the status of minorities in the country as only religious in nature. Article 260 of the constitution recognizes only religious minorities without acknowledging the various other minorities like linguistic and ethnic. The constitution of the Islamic Republic of Pakistan has authorized every citizen to have equal rights before the law in Article 25.

On the other hand, Article 36 protects all political rights of every citizen. The Constitution of Pakistan, 1973, reserved ten seats on separate electorate basis. In the similar manner, the religious minorities have a 5% reserved quota in jobs, and a 2% quota in higher education as well. However the reality is that these articles just pay lip service to the notions of rule of law and equality before law. In terms of implementation of these rights, especially for the minorities, it can be said that the constitution and the state have failed in protecting its minorities. The scholarship on the matter addresses these concerns by highlighting that granting equal opportunity to the minorities will not work as long as the local context allows them to exercise their rights.

## Segregation of Hindus

Discrimination of minorities begins as early as their school years, where they are treated as untouchables in the classrooms. Their fellow students eat food separately, verbally harass them by calling them impure and mocking their religion(Mehmood, Mirza, Khan, Shabbir, & Iqbal, 2014).

The Hindus are also demonized in the syllabi that is taught in the schools, ingraining children with such lies and biases about their fellow citizens. Continuous rise of religious intolerance and the inadequate response of political actors in the matter of minorities has gradually excluded the minorities from the decision making processes of the country. This is true for all the minority groups however what makes the situation of the hindus more worse off than their christian fellows is that they are not the 'people of the book'. This idea and notion of not being the Ahl al kitab, is not explicitly mentioned in legal texts but the local population keeps this in mind as far as their treatment of Hindus is concerned. Blasphemy laws passed during the dictatorial rule of General Zia ul Haq (1980-86) are another menace in the lives of the minorities of the country.

It has been observed that even upon the slightest allegation of blasphemy the worship places of minorities and their homes are destroyed within a blink. Such misuse of legal framework to haunt and dehumanize their own minority doesn't find parallel anywhere else in the region. The alleged blasphemy case of Asia Bibi is still present in the memory of the international civil society and the world. Hindus too have bore the brunt of these discriminatory laws against their places of worship and themselves. Another episode of violence is unleashed upon the Hindu minority of Pakistan when there are any major policy changes or riots with regards to muslims in India.

This trend of carrying out attacks on the Hindus in Pakistan in response to actions of India is a disturbing one. This furthers the sense of alienation in an already marginalized population of minorities. These acts signal that minorities of the country are no more than second class citizens. Regardless of what the constitution says they are to live with only as many rights as the society allows them. Coupled with the process of separate electorate where the member of the minority community cannot elect a person from the majority community and has to vote for the candidate from his community only. This method of election creates a chasm between the communities and further limits the possibility of integration between the communities in society.

## Way Forward For The Minorities and The State

The case study of Pakistani Hindus in the larger framework of South Asian human rights and minorities brings to light the complicated and frequently unsettling reality that the region's religious minority must contend with. The Hindu minority in Pakistan still faces systematic discrimination, social exclusion, and targeted violence despite international commitments and constitutional guarantees. These obstacles to the effective enjoyment of individual rights are made worse by sociopolitical factors, murky legal precedents, and cultural biases.

To address these concerns a receptive leadership is the need of the hour. Strong legislative foundations, efficient procedures for putting laws into practice, and a sincere political commitment to upholding and advancing the rights of minorities. In order to address the underlying causes of prejudice and violence against minorities, it also asks for increased regional collaboration and global attention. The global watchdogs responsible for reporting and addressing the concerns of minorities around the world should engage more seriously into the cases of gross human rights violation and misconduct. Furthermore, the long-term viability of human rights for every person in South Asia depends on promoting a culture of tolerance, inclusivity, and respect for variety.

The actions of the state against its own citizens should not go unnoticed and proper responsibility should be set through mounting pressure by the international community. A multimodal strategy incorporating governmental initiatives, legislative reforms, and societal transformation is needed to address these issues. The area can only hope to build a more just and equal society where everyone's rights are respected and upheld, regardless of their ethnicity or religion, by making consistent and coordinated efforts.

## *Conclusion*

The situation of the minorities in Pakistan remains bleak. With no legal recourse and inadequate political representation in the country, their hopelessness is justified. No help is available from the International community, and the institutional measures in the country are toothless to address these concerns. The rise of religious extremism in Pakistan and its promotion by successive governments, is a major factor in increasing the plight of the minorities in Pakistan.

Institutional integrity and an effort to create an inclusive policy for integration of minorities in the mainstream. In conclusion, this research aims to further the current conversation about minority rights by providing policy proposals that support the development of a more equitable and inclusive society. The article highlights the pressing need for comprehensive measures to preserve and enhance the rights of all minority communities in South Asia through a thorough examination of the difficulties Hindus in Pakistan confront. It seeks to open the door for a more egalitarian future where diversity is welcomed and everyone's human rights are respected by promoting increased awareness and action. This essay seeks to offer a thorough examination of the state of Hindus' human rights in Pakistan, taking into account both historical background and current conditions. It has explored the several kinds of violence and discrimination that the Hindu population faces, including problems with kidnappings, forced conversions, and socioeconomic marginalization. Additionally, the study looks at how state laws and regulations either exacerbate or lessen these problems.

## *Works Cited*

Zaidi, S. Akbar. "Religious minorities in Pakistan today." Journal of Contemporary Asia 18.4 (1988): 444 457.

Ali, A., Arslan, M., & Mustafa, G. (2022). Minorities Rights Protection in Punjab (Pakistan): A Comparative Analysis of Christians, Hindus and Sikhs. Annals of Human and Social Sciences, 3(2), 418-428.

Fuchs, M. M., & Fuchs, S. W. (2020). Religious minorities in Pakistan: Identities, citizenship and social belonging. South Asia: Journal of South Asian Studies, 43(1), 52-67.

# VI

# An Unequal Partition: Violence on Gendered Bodies Kamakshi Rautela

*Abstract*

The paper explores the nature of violence inflicted upon women's bodies during the Partition of 1947 that led to the formation of India and Pakistan. The article seeks to analyze the practice of engendered violence in pre-partition, during, and post-partition periods. Through this trajectory the following argument delves into the 'why' of violence- why one community raged against the other; why it is largely the women at the receiving end of the violence conducted by the state, family, and community; why honor of these stakeholder rest with the 'purity' of women's progenitive power; etc. To answer this, the paper focuses on the themes of violence, abduction, and recovery of women, widowhood, women's rehabilitation, agency, and the ever-changing identity of women. Additionally, it discusses how the state and community remember the partition and its impact on women in the present context.

**Keywords:** religious masculinities, martyrological culture, permissible violence, rehabilitation and recovery programme, deterritorialization and reterritorialization of women's bodies, and biopower

## Introduction

According to Jalal (2013), the 1947 Partition is regarded as "the central historical event in twentieth-century South Asia" leading to the formation of two states- India and Pakistan. The paper aims to transcend this monotonous understanding of the partition as a mere event that led to the creation of the states by focusing on women's experiences during the partition, and how women's bodies were a 'territory' to practice 'religious masculinities' by the communities (Dandekar, 2021), and 'patriarchal codes' by the states. The following analysis of violence on women's bodies will focus on the region of western India and West Pakistan.

The first section examines the 'why' of violence, i.e., the motives behind the violence among the Sikh, Hindu, and Muslim during the partition, questioning whether it stemmed from grievances or greed.

The second section delves into the violence against women's bodies during the partition, including atrocities by 'other' community, their 'own' community, and by women themselves or what I call self-destruction.

The third section focuses on the state's role in exacerbating women's suffering through its 'recovery' and 'rehabilitation' programs, particularly for abducted women and 'unattached' women, where it acts as the "maai-baap" (mother-father) of these women. Some attention would also be given to the experiences of Dalit women. The section seeks to answer why for states recovery operation was necessary, and whether women had agency?

The fourth section examines how women impacted by partition grapple with identity issues after the partition and how their bodies are remembered by the state and community in contemporary periods, highlighting how gendered bodies become markers of division between states and communities.

## UNDERSTANDING THE CONTEXT OF VIOLENCE

The partition of 1947 caused massive migration and violence, particularly in Punjab, as governments were unprepared for the consequences (Tripathy, 2014 ). One factor that fueled inter-community violence is grievance, rooted in the colonized past. According to feminist historian, Urvashi Butalia (1998), the "territorial murder," by British imperialism was the cause of the ire of people in both communities. The partition was seen as unfair because many important religious sites for Sikhs and Muslims were divided by borders. Hindus also have historical ties to certain areas, such as Lahore. Furthermore, the predicament of the populace was exacerbated by issues with employment, livelihood, and homelands— eventually, gave rise to competition, leading to the internalization of violence (Fanon, 1963). This suppressed rage when not directed at colonizers, turned inward, leading oppressed communities to violence against those they had shared historical ties with.

Additionally, the greed of two key political organizations- the Muslim League and the Indian National Congress, eager for power after election victories, hastened the partition without considering the views of those affected. INC even considered partition as a 'necessity' of independence (Butalia, 1998).

Nevertheless, there was the existence of 'latent' violence between communities, rooted in deep-seated antagonism stemming from economic disparities, discriminatory practices, and past Muslim rule. This 'latent violence' (Galtung, 1969) intensified with partition, leading to what can be termed as "retributive genocide," where communities sought revenge based on selective memory of historical grievances. (Brass, 2003). Retribution was also fueled by cultural nationalism, as communities asserted their unique identities, such as Sikh identity was based on the 'martyrological' culture associated with their Gurus. Thus, the partition of India-Pakistan serves as an example of "nationalist fratricide" shaped by a complex interplay of historical memory, identity politics, and communal tensions (Menon & Bhasin, 1998).

In this context of communal violence, women's bodies were being used as symbols to define the "self" and the "other." Their bodies symbolized breaking the borders of religion and politics (Menon & Bhasin, 1998) where the attack on women was assumed as an attack on the honor of their communities, challenging men's masculine roles as protectors, and feminizing them.

## *VIOLENCE DURING PARTITION*

The partition of 1947 witnessed severe instances of violence against women's bodies, perpetrated by men from 'other' communities, from their 'own' community, and even by women themselves.

By male of 'other' community

Sexual violence committed by males of the 'other' community has a wide range of devastating effects, with acts such as branding them with "Pakistan Zindabad" and "Hindustan Zindabad", and tattooing women in religious spaces being particularly egregious. These acts were meant to humiliate women by engraving the division of British India on their bodies (Saxena, 2014). Additionally, brutal acts like amputating women's breasts symbolized distorting their 'femininity' and ability to nurture, effectively erasing their connection to their 'own' community. Similarly, rape, a form of 'ethnic cleansing', was used to obliterate the future generations of a particular group (Butalia, 1998) by 'contaminating' their bloodline and undermining their reproductive power. It was also used to feminize men who failed to protect their female relatives (Misri, 2011).

One such incident has been accounted in Menon & Bhasin's (1998) which involved the brutal attack on a Muslim Girls' Hostel in Amritsar, where inmates were stripped, raped, and murdered in public. Perpetrators of violent acts attributed their actions to the intensity of the situation for which they 'remorse' later on. Such violence reflects the influence of extremists' form of religious understanding, diminishing individuals' mental potentialities and causing psychological violence, later on (Galtung, 1969). Furthermore, such religion-based violence challenges the border solution offered by the states that failed to acknowledge that violence doesn't respect boundaries, and, partition was the beginning of the problem (Butalia, 1998).

By males of their 'own' community and by women themselves

Another category of gendered violence has been conducted by male relatives from women's 'own' communities, a form of "intrafamilial violence" (Bacchetta, 2000) which has been portrayed as "permissible violence" (Menon & Bhasin, 1998). In South Asian society, historical traditions have glorified women who sacrifice their lives for honor as martyrs. Indian culture idealizes motherhood as contributing to the nation's cause, thus, motherhood through being veeraprasabini; wifehood through practices like Sati and Jauhar, and womanhood through Shakti and Birangona in wars. These patriarchal notions emphasized that a woman's destiny and happiness are only achievable through these ideals (Tripathy, 2014 ).

Similarly, in the Sindh region of Pakistan, honor killing, known as kara kori, reflects deeply ingrained cultural norms. The Sikh community also has a tradition of martyrdom consciousness, passed down through narratives of suffering and valor during the Jallianwala Bagh Massacre. During the partition, these ideals persisted, with death associated with pride and fear seen as dishonorable (Butalia, 1998).

One such account of honor killing during partition has been recorded in Menon & Bhasin (1998) where a man killed his daughters when advised by his Muslim neighbors to marry his daughters to their sons for safety. This extreme act was driven by the belief that women were at risk of being converted and impregnated by men of another religion, bringing 'impurity' to their community. Therefore, women could "save" their communities by sacrificing themselves through honor killings, reflecting lack of women's agency women whose consensus had not been taken.

Besides this, women violate their own bodies. In the Rawalpindi region, there have been cases where women have chosen to drown in a well to protect their honor. However, it's difficult to determine if this was a choice, given the deeply ingrained concept of shame and honor. Women may have internalized patriarchal beliefs and perceive a 'forced death' as a voluntary sacrifice (Menon & Bhasin, 1998; Butalia, 1998; Saxena, 2014). Moreover, the 'sacrificial violence' was even glorified, evident in The Statesman newspaper of April 15, 1947, which reported, that through the Rawalpindi incident, women revived the Jauhar tradition and followed Gandhi's advice that sometimes suicide is morally superior to submission (Butalia, 1998). Thus, those who did not choose to die honorably were shamed (Menon & Bhasin, 1998), showing how willingness to use violence became a way for communities to assert their belongingness. Thus, violence and community became intertwined during the Partition, each reinforcing the other's importance (Pandey, 1997).

## *STATE-BASED VIOLENCE: SCENES FROM POST-PARTITION*

This section is based on the understanding that the state is not always a security-provider as during, the post-partition period, it jeopardized women's security by regulating their bodies and identities through the categorisation of women as abducted women and 'unattached' women. These categories then determined the women's identity and government policies on recovery and restoration.

Abducted Women

During partition some were sold off to different individuals, some women were brainwashed and became perpetrators themselves, and many were manipulated by maulvis who portrayed a negative image of India, instilling fear in their minds to facilitate conversion (Butalia, 1998). These acts were based upon the understanding that by raping, converting, marrying, and indoctrinating, a lethal attack has been launched against the 'other' community as women were comprehended as the 'blind spot' of any community.

However, after the partition, many women were reported missing, and states made efforts to retrieve them by signing an Inter-Dominion Agreement in 1947, leading to the establishment of the Central Recovery Operation. The idea was to bring back 'home' women who were living with men of 'other' religion (Menon & Bhasin, 1998; Butalia, 1998). The term 'home' is contested in this situation, since for states 'home' was aligned with religious territoriality, while for women this was not the case.

The Abducted Persons (Recovery and Restoration) Bill was passed in 1949, defining 'abducted person' based on a fixed date, i.e. March 1, 1947. Marriages or conversions after this date would be labeled as 'illegal'. The women had no agency in the matter, even if they protested or had genuine relationships (Butalia, 1998). Thus, women were not going back to their 'home' but actually bidding farewell to the home, forcefully, where their sense of belonging lay.

Furthermore, the Act allowed police officers to search for abducted persons without a warrant and established a tribunal to determine their status where the latter could not challenge their detention in court. Also, the government and authorities involved in implementing the Act were protected from legal actions (Menon & Bhasin, 1993).

Both the Recovery Operation and The Abducted Persons Bill need to be critically understood. Firstly, the way the state was asserting control and ownership over these women reflects a patriarchal society with the state assuming a protective father figure, to preserve the honor of the motherland, which is symbolized by a woman's body (Menon & Bhasin, 1998). By imposing the notion of motherhood upon the sexuality and chastity of the women, which was seen as defiled due to abduction and rape, the state prioritized restoring the perceived 'purity' of the nation, disregarding their preferences and choices. This resonates with Gayatri Spivak's understanding of women being denied a voice, wherein others speak on their behalf. Thus, both the operation and the bill failed to provide 'true' emancipation, where women can freely exercise their right to choose.

The state's patriarchal obsession with the notion of 'purity' is evident when it uses Hindu symbolism and manipulates religious narratives-portraying abducted women as Sita to emphasize their purity. However, the state used the notion of 'purity' in another way, this time by challenging gender norms while depicting menstruation as 'purifying' (Bacchetta, 2000). This has been done due to the anxiety among abducted women of not being accepted back into their religion and community due to the perceived impurity (Menon & Bhasin, 1998; Butalia, 1998).

Secondly, religion was not only used to 'reterritorialize' Sikh and Hindu women's bodies but also to 'deterritorialize' Muslim women's bodies back to Pakistan, despite India's claim of being secular. The bill denied the abducted women legal rights and protections, labeling their marriages as 'illegal' and their children as 'illegitimate', and transporting them across borders without consent and with a limited chance to appeal (Menon & Bhasin, 1993). I consider this 'recovery' process as 'barter of women' which was not monetary but indeed religious and where women were relegated to the status of 'chattel' (Butalia, 1998). Moreover, the notion of 'illegitimacy' stems from the importance placed on the concept of 'rightful belonging' to a family, community, or nation whose sanctity can only be preserved by keeping sexuality away from secularity. This is the main reason for mass abortion program (Menon & Bhasin, 1998).

This shows that there is a complex power dynamics between gender, community, and nation, with a general patriarchal consensus on how to control women's sexuality.

## *"Unattached Women":*

Another priority of the state was the "unattached women", particularly those who became widows during the violence of the partition. The Indian state committed to providing lifelong support for 'war widows' and temporary assistance for unattached women until they could regain self-sufficiency. Thus, the state took on a role similar to that of a nurturing maa in providing rehabilitation and welfare programs for these women, a form of 'benign paternalism', and not that of a protected father – as in the case of abducted women (Menon & Bhasin, 1998).

In December 1947, the state adopted a resolution outlining its 'moral' responsibilities towards refugee women- mental empowerment, providing employment, education, and skill-enhancement (Menon & Bhasin, 1998).The state aimed to help them become economically independent. But this welfare role should be examined critically.

Firstly, the rehabilitation efforts reflect the colonial mentality of 'civility' based on women's status in society. In the British period the state through its efforts to ban 'sati' and 'child marriages' considered it as a way of 'civilizing' Indian society. This continued in the post-partition period when the Indian state contrasted itself with Pakistan as a more "civilized" state that rendered social justice through the rehabilitation program (Butalia, 1998). Thus, women's bodies became the debate of civility between the states.

Secondly, the rehabilitation program was not very effective in addressing women's economic struggles, exploitation, and low wages. Social worker, Damyanti Sahgal revealed to Butalia that despite reports of sufficient earnings, women were still struggling to survive due to lack of education which made them unable to challenge exploitation (Butalia, 1998). Moreover, government attempts to separate women from their children, as it labeled them 'illegitimate', was an additional struggle. Thus, physical rehabilitation neglected the emotional, educational, and psychological needs of women.

Thus, I assert that women were bestowed with biological citizenship, whether abducted or 'unattached', as their biological status of whether being impregnated by 'other' community, had 'illegitimate' marriages, or remained 'sexually inactive' due to their husbands' death during the partition, were important which then linked to their religious identity. However, this understanding of citizenship does not apply to lower-class/ caste women, they had different experiences. Particularly, Dalit women continued to be socially marginalized and faced violence from upper-caste men who believed they had the right to violate the bodies of these women because they were seen as 'impure'.

The state's neglect further worsened their situation by denying them refuge and excluding them from 'welfare' projects. Thus, some Dalit women used the chaos of partition to challenge caste-class boundaries, improving their social status. This experience may have strengthened their collective Dalit identity amidst intercaste-class dynamics across borders (Bacchetta, 2000). Thus, the partition reshaped physical, national, community (Menon & Bhasin, 1998), and social identities.

The analysis reveals that the objectification and control of women's bodies by the state and society is a longstanding and heterogeneous issue that is influenced by factors such as caste, race, and class where some bodies matter more.

## *TO WHICH NATION WOMEN BELONG?*

The question of women's belonging is complex due to the changing nature of their identities. Do they identify more with the nation of their birth or the nation that formed after partition? Is their sense of belonging tied to religion or territory? It is challenging to determine which identity women prioritize, as their status has been indeterminate throughout the history of partition. Nevertheless, above made analysis shows that 'belonging' for women is determined by their acceptance and legitimacy in the eyes of the state, family, and community, and is tied to their purity and loyalty (Menon & Bhasin, 1998). This is evident in the 19th-century Arya Samaj's Shuddhi program, which aimed to 'repurify' converted individuals, especially women, by reintegrating them into their religious communities. Such reintegration practices continued in the post-partition period in the form of violence, recovery, rehabilitation, mass abortion, and mass marriages.

Moreover, women's inclusion in the nation is also influenced by factors, such as viewing the nation as female, the distinction between public and private spaces, and the role of women in preserving cultural and ethnic identities. In India, legislation on marriage, divorce, and inheritance is used to uphold patriarchal control and prioritize male authority. The Muslim Women's (Protection of Rights in Divorce) Bill of 1986 is an instance of the state ignoring women's rights for the sake of communal well-being. Another example is of BJP-led NDA government who has exploited women's bodies for political gains by using metaphors like "India's daughters" of the partition period for Indian women rescued from Pakistan since 2014, an attempt to connect their actions with a historical event and to reinforce a Hindu-centric identity for India (Dandekar, 2021).

On the other hand, the community, through rituals of remembrance that take place in gurudwaras of Delhi promotes the idea of an ideal woman by portraying women's suicides as heroic and sacrifices for the community. Thus, dismiss any personal agency and keep them within the private sphere (Butalia, 1998).

Thus, in this context women belong to a nation constituted by the community which imposes cultural norms in the private sphere, and by the state which imposes a nationalist identity on women in public sphere, restricting their rights within a façade democratic set-up.

## *CONCLUSION*

The representation of violated women's bodies in the nation's discourse can be placed within Foucault's concept of biopower which explains how nation-states govern their populations through the regulation of bodies and the production of compliant subjects. In the case of raped and abducted women, both India and Pakistan limited women's agency through disciplinary power at the individual level- by imposing norms and expectations associated with women's bodies- and regulatory power at the state level by using policies and rehabilitation programs which further reinforce gendered identities and expectations (Munawar, et al., 2013), as seen in the organization of abortion programs and marriages for recovered women. Thus, a complex interplay of power dynamics, societal norms, and state control over women's lives.

## *Works Cited*


Anon., n.d. wikipedia. [Online]
Available at: https://en.wikipedia.org/wiki/Partition_of_India#Independence,_migration,_and_violence

Bacchetta, P., 2000. Reinterrogating Partition Violence: Voices of Women/Children/Dalits in India's Partition. Feminist Studies, pp. 556-585.

Brass, P. R., 2003. The partition of India and retributive genocide in the Punjab, 1946-47: Means, methods, and purposes 1. Journal of Genocide Research 5, pp. 71-101.

Butalia, U., 1998. Other Side of Silence: Voices from the Partition of India. s.l.:Penguin.

Dandekar, D., 2021. Women's 'Retrieval' from Pakistan: 'India's Daughters' and the Emotional History of Partition. South Asia: Journal of South Asian Studies, pp. 703-720.

Fanon, F., 1963. The Wretched of the Earth. New York: Grove Press.

Galtung, J., 1969. Violence, Peace and Peace Research. Journal of Peace Research, pp. 167-191.

Jalal, A., 2013. The Pity of Partition: Manto's Life, Times, and Work across the India-Pakistan Divide. s.l.:Harper Collins .

Menon, R. & Bhasin, K., 1993. Recovery, Rupture, Resistance: Indian State and Abduction of Women during Partition. Economic and Political Weekly, pp. WS2-WS11.

Menon, R. & Bhasin, K., 1998. Borders and Boundaries: Women in India's Partition. New Brunswick, New Jersey: Rutger University Press.

Misri, D., 2011. The Violence of Memory: Renarrating Partition Violence in Shauna Singh Baldwin's What the Body Remembers. Meridians , pp. 1-25.

Munawar, R. et al., 2013. Female Sexuality as Carrier of Masculinity: A Feminist Critique of History of Sub Continent Partition (1947). European Academic Research , pp. 2167-2175.

Pandey, G., 1997. Community and Violence: Recalling Partition. Economic and Political Weekly, pp. 2037-2039+ 2041-2045.

Saxena, C., 2014. ON RELIGION AND ITS IMPLICATIONS ON WOMEN DURING PARTITION OF INDIA. Proceedings of the Indian History Congress, pp. 1253-1271.

Tripathy, A., 2014 . History is a Woman's Body: A Study of Some Partition Narratives, Odisha: s.n.

# VII

# Cross Border Crimes Arising out of growing concern across Indo Myanmar Border Relations  Julia Jose

Recently we observed Indian diplomat speaking on human rights situation in Myanmar during 56th regular session of human rights council which began on 18th of June till 12th of July 2024.Myanmar has been engulfed in conflict since military coup in the year 2021.This has resulted in immense lashes between military junta and resistance forces. The instability has implications for northeastern states like Manipur and Mizoram. Post military coup across the border we have seen illegal narcotics, arms smuggling and human trafficking as challenges. Previously, we have seen with no other source of income how the local population were compelled to get involved with drug traffickers. Many a times drug traffickers were supported by KMT forces, Burmese communist insurgents and secessional frontier tribes for it's the only way to sustain the income.

*Background*

Arab traders came up with opium on the shores of Myanmar in the 16th century. Until 1800, Opium was impacting the lower class. The production of opium began to increase with increase in international opium trade. However, it was only after the second world war that a large-scale flow of drugs started in the region. 1949 Mao banned opium production in China so it shifted from China's Yunnan province to Myanmar's shan state. Time and again, we did see a fall in the production of opium but in the meantime a rise in methamphetamines and production of other synthetic drugs.

The two months after the military reinstated its turbulent rule have seen a sharp increase in criminal activity in Myanmar, creating significant difficulties for the region's attempts to manage cross-border crime. The border between India and Myanmar has garnered attention lately due to military operations by the Myanmar government against opposition organisations. Numerous security concerns have been brought up by the ongoing operation, both inside the nation and with its neighbours. The most crucial cross-border crimes include Arms smuggling, Drugs Trafficking, and Human trafficking.

## *Key drivers*

The primary key driver is cultural and traditional unity amongst the minority groups which has led to lack of unity to tackle the country's serious problems. Secondly geography and climate- Northeastern part of Myanmar being part of Golden triangle possess favourable condition for cultivation of opium. The third key driver is the kind of Government in Myanmar and fourthly economy which we can call black and grey market to get the goods from outside the region and outside the country and finally the influence of international environment in fostering the growth of opium production or drug economy.

## *Cross Border Crimes*

The Golden crescent of southwest Asia comprises Pakistan, Afghanistan and the Golden triangle includes Myanmar, Thailand and Laos. Both of them are leading opium poppy producers of the world. North Eastern India lies close to what is referred to as the Golden Triangle. It is said that the Military junta sponsors drug trade for a source of revenue. When countries like Indonesia, Malaysia and Singapore became serious about drug trafficking, they came up with effective measures to deal with the same. Manipur came across as an alternative route for drug trade as it lies close to the Golden Triangle. Burmese heroin is transported from Burmese town thamu to Manipur through the border zone of Moreh.

Drug trade and drug use are leading to HIV AIDS in Manipur. Looking at the alarming condition the state government came up with a ban on drugs under the Prevention of Narcotic and Psychotropic Drug abuse act of 1985. The ban further led to an increase in the case of HIV as sharing of needles became a common thing due to unavailability of them. Some of the reasons for increased use of drugs are a large youth population, Westernised values, free lifestyle, widespread unemployment and lack of future prospects.

The instability in Myanmar had led to arms trafficking across the border .During an operation that happened on the year 31st December 2021, Security forces recovered a large quantity of explosives from an area three kilometres south of Mawhere village in Saiha district along India Myanmar international border. The recoveries include 94 kilograms of belox granules, 395 kilograms of Gelatin rods,356 rounds of 12gauge shotgun, 70 mm cartridges, one impoverished explosive device, lead acid battery, two detonators and other materials including foreign communication equipment.

Security forces recovered ammunition near Tiau Kai village in Champhai District along India Myanmar international border in the year 23rd October 2021. The recoveries near the Tiau Kai village entail 100 live rounds, 38 Neogel Gelatin stocks and 251 detonators. Security forces even recovered one rifle along with one live round of ammunition from the Chhungte area of Champai district in the year 9th September 2021.

The instability in Myanmar has created an environment for Human trafficking in the Indo Myanmar border. As stated by V.Muraleedharan, Ministry of state of external affairs, more than 400 Indian men in fraudulent IT jobs are struck in Myanmar. This issue was also highlighted by the Indian external affairs minister when he met Myanmar counterpart during Mekong Ganga cooperation in Bangkok. There are a lot of challenges in addressing the human trafficking issue. The Myawaddy region, where trafficking comes as the worst, is located in Myanmar's Kayin's province .In this region, armed militia holds greater control which limits the control of the Myanmar military government. As a result, it comes as really difficult to rescue the stranded Indians.

## *Measures*

The decision to construct fencing all along the border of Manipur and Myanmar was due to security reasons because strict patrolling is not possible all along the border considering the geographical conditions like harsh terrain. India was forced to take certain measures to ensure that the porous border does not become an easy passage for the insurgents, flow of arms and drugs. During 2001- 2003, the Indian security forces were of the opinion that the porous border was responsible for the death of 200 security forces and civilians in the region. Fencing along the border can be seen as an effort to concretise the part of the border as de facto demarcation lines. Construction of barbed wire along the border to address the issue of drug trafficking, irregular immigration and human trafficking.

But if we consider the border line communities it is something that will impact the kinship ties that both the communities share across the border. People on both the sides of the border are engaged in economic and social exchanges from time to time. Fencing means people to people ties will get impacted. It means severing the age old ties and isolation of India from the rest of the world. Historically, people across the border had no other choice than to depend on each other to meet their daily needs. There are positive measures taken across the border region like opening of border haats, Friendship road and Asian highway to strengthen the economic ties across the border regions.

## *Conclusion*

Therefore it is crucial to address the grievances arising out of border fencing, capitalise on shared bonds that borderland communities share with each other. The direct outcome of military junta in Myanmar comes out to be increase in cross border crimes like drug trafficking, Human trafficking and arms smuggling which can only be addressed with different regions across the globe cooperating with each other and providing necessary aids to tackle the growing concern. To address the social challenge in the region is of utmost importance as it is one of the root cause for dependence in drugs as alternative source of income. Once we address the drug trafficking many other issues could be addressed like arms trafficking and human trafficking.

Fencing across the border is again considered as solution which again should be implemented taking into consideration the natives across the borderlands. Exchange of enclaves under land boundary agreement can be considered as one way to deal with the growing concern in Indo Myanmar region as it came as a success for India Bangladesh.

## *Works Cited*


i. Suwal al Jangu, Debate intensifies over scrapping of free movement regime on India- Myanmar border, The Hindu, February 08, 2024.

ii. Mizoram Assessment-2024, South Asian Terrorism Portal,2024.

iii. Prem Mahadevan, Crossing the line, Geopolitics and criminality at the India-Myanmar border, November 2020.

iv. Zo Tum Hmung, Time is running out for India's Balancing Act on the Myanmar border, United States Institute of Peace, June 20023.

v. Krishna Mohan Mishra, Terrorist planning to infiltrate India via Myanmar, DNA, December 23, 2021.

vi. Saket Ambarkhane and Sanjay Valentine, Over a year later, Myanmar's Military Coup Threatens India's National Security, United States Institute of Peace, May 10, 2022.

vii. Niranjan Marjani, India Faces a Two-Front Challenge from Post-Coup Myanmar, The Diplomat, April 26, 2023.

viii. Sreeparna Banerjee, India-Myanmar: Escalating human trafficking concerns, ORF, August 01, 2023

ix. Murali Krishnan, What is India's relationship to Myanmar's Military Junta, Down Earth, February 08, 2022.

x. Rishi Gupta, How China and India are handling Myanmar crisis three years on, Think China, February 29, 2024.

xi. Aparna Pande, India's Realpolitik Myanmar Policy, GIS, October 26, 2023.

xii. Fiona Raval, Lost Bets: Rethinking India's Myanmar Strategy, IPCS, December 27, 2023.

xiii. Lindsay Maizland, Myanmar's Troubled History: Coups, Military rule, and ethnic conflict, Council on Foreign Relations, January 31, 2022.

xiv. Pierre Gottschlich, The India- Myanmar Relationship: New Directions after a Change of Governments? IQAS.

xv. Rajiv Bhatia, India Myanmar Relations, Changing Contours, Routledge,2016

xvi. Maria Elena Sassaroli, Drugs flow where the rivers meet: Myanmar's drug economy before and after the coup

xvii K Saroj Kumar Sharma, Influx Of Myanmarese Into Northeast Matter of Concern: India to UN,June 21,2024.

xviii. Rimli Basu,Guns, Drugs and the Mystery of Indo Myanmar Relations,JSTOR,2008.

xix. Munmun Majumdar, India Myanmar Border Fencing and India's Act East Policy,SAGE, March 2020

xx. Ningthoujam Koiremba Singh and William Nunes, Drug Trafficking and Narco-Terrorism as security threats: A study of India's North East,SAGE,March 2013

# VIII

# Transitional Gender Justice: Addressing LGBTQI+ Concerns in Postwar Human Rights Activism Swetarupa Mishra

The literature on transitional justice shows enough concerns about binaries such as victim-oppressor, conflict-post conflict, and as the question puts it-catalyst-product dichotomy as well. My essay shall focus on comprehending the nuances of moving beyond these binaries and understanding transitional justice and sustainable political transition as complementary to each other while ranging between factors of which being a catalyst and a product are a part. I shall attempt to do this by streamlining my argument towards the scarce representation of gender minorities in transitional justice and political transition both in epistemology and practice and highlight why their inclusion in transitional justice is necessary.

I am focusing on Lebanon and Columbia for this purpose as these are the two places on which there were exactly two pieces of literature written that catered to LGBTQI rights and conditions in relation to transitional justice and political transition. I shall draw on these case studies by interacting with the literature theorizing transition and justice.

*Is transitioning to democracy the solution? What is the kind of democracy we have in*

*picture and in practice?*

In the Lebanese context, John Nagle writes, "the war had a hardening effect on sectarian identities, a process that was exacerbated by 'mass displacement, wide-scale killing, rape, torture, arbitrary detention, and enforced disappearances. The civil war officially ended with the Ta'if Peace Agreement in 1989….Ta'if's title – 'no victor and no vanquished' – signified that peace is achieved by creating an institutional apparatus that ensured no group could dominate the state. The key institutional mechanism to freeze the balance of power between the main groups was power sharing" (Nagle, 2019).

Lebanon calling itself a democracy can be characterized under what Carothers calls the 'Grey Zone' which includes countries that "have some attributes of democratic political life, including at least limited political space for opposition parties and independent civil society, as well as regular elections and democratic constitutions. Yet they suffer from serious democratic deficits" (Carothers, 2002). However, it is interesting to note that Lebanon and many such Middle Eastern and South Asian countries are being viewed from the west especially, US liberal democratic ideals. While Carothers tries his best to address that, he ends up rooting for countries' transition to democracies, therefore asserting that the 'white man's burden' and democracy being the end goal of transformation and transition of any conflict-ridden society.

A lot of attention has been paid to elections as a defining characteristic of democracy. In Reconsidering Transition Paradigm, Diamond says, "I think the transition simply ends when the basic definition of democracy is achieved: a regime in which people can choose and replace their leaders in reasonably free and fair elections, with a minimal surrounding climate of freedoms as well as accountability in between elections" ((Diamond et al., 2014). Such oversimplification of what a successful democracy looks like renders the very much present gendered and sexualised factors invisible to its formation.

The example can be found in Lebanon as Nagle writes, "Postwar Lebanese elections have led to 'hardening, rather than ameliorating, sectarian cleavages. Endemic state weaknesses are deliberately maintained by sectarian elites so that goods and services are placed under their administrative networks. These social welfare services – especially healthcare and education – are used to ensure that much of the working-class population are heavily reliant on the assistance provided by their communal leaders" (Nagle, 2019).

Such features of Lebanese democracy calls to question the birth factors of the same as they can determine its durability as well (Diamond et. al, 2014) In order to remember its birth, one needs to consider historical memory. Historical memory as Horowitz points out, is of two types- "good recollections and recollections of what you'd like to avoid" (Diamond et al., 2014). This categorization becomes pertinent from a queer feminist lens in reference to -if the memories of gendered minorities are included in that distinction?

How far are their issues, and conditions recorded in memorialisation that comes to influence transition and transitional justice? As a response to this Maier writes, "Very few documents produced post-armed conflict even mention sexual and gender minorities let alone describe efforts made to include them in a resolution process." This lack of data renders the mechanism of 'uncovering the truth' helpless which hampers the process of transitional justice and this in turn affects political transition where the society which has not recovered from past traumas continues to survive through that accumulation of violence, trauma, and silencing as we see in the case of Lebanon with the sectarian government and personal status laws barring
experiences of LGBTQI community. How then can transition be reconfigured from the perspective of its victims?

## *Victimization and transformative transitional justice:*

The term victim here stirs up a debate on who is called a victim and who gets to decide the same? While Madlingozi provides some insightful contributions to this discourse, the gendered aspect of it needs further investigation. Madlingozi writes, "Given the fact that transitional justice experts legitimize their existence on the basis of speaking about and for victims, is it ever possible for the expert to exercise 'responsibility' to the victim's story in ways that contribute to the genuine empowerment of the victim?" ((Madlingozi, 2010) ).

Here, the categorization of victim and survivor is important, and it is imperative to study how gender plays in this categorization and in who makes this categorization. Maier writes about Columbia that, "The use of LGBTI as a category in this way conflates gender identity and sexual orientation. It is, therefore, possible that a victim who identifies as a lesbian woman would only be categorized as a woman and excluded from the statistics for LGBTI victims. The nexus of victimization and intersectionality of identities presents a unique challenge for societies engaging in peacebuilding" (Maier, 2019).

This resonates with Boesten and Wilding when they state that, "transitional justice has an obligation to look at ameliorating the structures underlying this violence, whether they be the institutions, norms and values, economic relations or family structures that shape people's experiences, choices and opportunities. We argue, therefore, that the macro and formal processes that constitute existing elite-driven, formal transitional justice mechanisms exclude, by design, the complexity of gendered experiences" (Boesten & Wilding, 2015). With this in view, if the political transition occurs, the transitional justice position is questioned. Can the transition be complete with such inequalities unaddressed in societies? Therefore, both political transition and transitional justice perform neither as catalyst nor as products in relation to each other but the lack of a nuanced understanding that includes gender posits them dysfunctional, irrespective of the binary framework they are placed in as per the question.

The other aspect of Madlingozi's statement caters to the responsibility towards victims and their story can be analyzed alongside the literature on transformational transitional justice. He writes, "'Responsibility to the story' should mean more than being nice to victims or adhering to rigorous scientific and ethical standards; it should also, if not principally, be about redistribution of resources and power" (Madlingozi, 2010).

Gready and Robins proceed on similar lines as they define transformative justice as "transformative change that emphasizes local agency and resources, the prioritization of process rather than preconceived outcomes and the challenging of unequal and intersecting power relationships and structures of exclusion at both the local and the global level" (Gready & Robins, 2014). Therefore, it addresses chronic structural violence and unequal social relations. They define transformative justice through a holistic prism which challenges the dichotomy of peace vs justice by including both judicial and non-judicial measures in the arena of transformative transitional justice.

As long as its applicability is concerned the coexistence of transition and transformation hasn't been possible especially with reference to Lebanon when it comes to gender minorities. This is suffced by Nagle as he writes, "Sexuality is also regulated by the sectarian apparatus. Law 534 of the Penal Code, which is used to enforce the status laws, criminalizes sex deemed as 'unnatural', is directed at the LGBTQI population, and it carries a minimum one-year jail sentence. Expressions of non-conforming gender identity are further prosecuted under several other articles regulating public morality" (Nagle, 2019). So, when such stringent laws oppress a whole category of the population, how can the transition be called just and where can we find any trace of transformation in this transition?

Additionally, the texts by both Madlingozi; Gready and Robins does not engage with gender minorities. In Gready and Robin's piece, gender is just reduced to a section in their whole discourse about transformative justice. This alarming scarcity calls for an epistemological evaluation in terms of gender representation in literature concerning transitional and transformative justice.

## Why the need for a Queer Feminist Analysis?

The conceptualization of gender justice in transformative transitional justice is somewhat dealt with by Boester and Wilding. Through their writing, they engage with women and intersectionality in post war societies, but they fail to include other gender minorities in their analysis. However, in their concluding point they highlight this concern when they write, "By and large, while gender studies and feminist critique have indicated the need for a relational and intersectional understanding of gender, the term is applied so as to equal women (Hudson, 2010 p.50)

Since such an interpretation does nothing for an understanding of gender inequality as a societal problem, this way of applying 'gender' to international policy and law tends to reproduce harmful binaries and stereotypes that only reinforce the inequality that is supposedly being challenged (Frank 2006; Campbell 2007; O'Rourke, 2011; Sjoberg, 2011)." (Boesten & Wilding, 2015). Their concluding point substantiates my argument for the scarce literature that addresses concerns of gender minorities and engages with their role in transitional justice.

Building on the necessity of a queer feminist lens of inclusion of marginalized gender identities in transitional justice, Fobear and Baines write, "Queer bodies have long been thought of as a threat to social stability and public order. This is particularly evident in areas transitioning from a period of mass violence, such as genocide, conflict, state-repression, slavery and settler colonialism, when LGBTI populations become easy targets for state and public violence" (Fobear & Baines, 2020).

Lebanon's sectarian system is deeply intertwined with gender and sexuality. The sects follow 15 separate laws regulating the personal status of their members, and each sect receives state funding to operate its own religious courts to adjudicate cases related to marriage, divorce, custody of children, and inheritance (Nagle, 2019). Therefore, it is evident that Fobear and Baines words hold true for Lebanon and many such transitioning nations where queer bodies have been criminalized.

In Lebanon, as Fobear and Baines point out, "Activists in Helem–the first recognised LGBTI rights group in the Middle East and North Africa–navigate between postwar sectarian institutions that are not accessible to them and global human rights policies that are available, but not necessarily applicable in the local context. These local LGBTI actors confront deeply entrenched structural and agential barriers that afford little opportunities for advancing LGBTI rights and policy change" (Fobear & Baines, 2020). Therefore, the inclusion of marginalised sexual and gender minorities in a transformative gender approach towards transitional justice will enhance the scope of the field and add to a positive correlation between political and transitional justice as product and catalyst in each other's making. Columbia's way of addressing LGBTQI victims and survivors of armed conflict gives hope for the future.

## *Way forward: The Exemplary Case of Columbia*

Colombia suffered a civil war that lasted over 50 years. Over the last 30 plus years, Colombia has had a handful of start-and-stop peace talks with two of its most prominent guerrilla groups (Maier, 2019). In terms of their gender inclusive transitional justice approach, they launched a collaborative project titled 'Assessing and promoting access by LGBTI victims of the armed conflict to transitional justice mechanisms.' Maier writes, "It consisted of two regional workshops and one national forum. The working session explored topics such as the current state of the peace process, what are LGBTI organizations doing and how, who are the actors, key issue areas for the LGBTI population, and a discussion of what LGBTI victims have and what they want.

The proposed outcome of these three events was the design of an advocacy plan to raise awareness of the violations committed by illegal armed groups against members of the LGBTI community and improve their access to transitional justice mechanisms, particularly truth-seeking and memory initiatives" (Maier, 2019).

Maier also mentions Carolina, a lesbian woman who was also a women's rights activist and was a victim of the war. Maier writes, "Carolina's story circled around whether she was targeted for being a woman, being an activist for women's rights, or for being a lesbian.

The interconnectedness of identities made this story even more complex and highlighted the multiple levels of vulnerabilities one can experience within the context of Colombia's armed conflict" (Maier, 2019). The field of transitional justice desperately needs inclusion of such multiple levels of oppression one experiences under vulnerabilities of marginalized identities. On 7 & 8 April 2016 Caribe Afirmativo, in partnership with a German foundation, held the first citizen forum in Colombia for historically discriminated groups and the peace process. This forum took place in Cartagena and Barranquilla intending to discover how armed conflict furthered their experience of exclusion and denial of rights (Maier, 2019). It is important to note that these initiatives were by civil society organizations thereby stressing on the importance of networks (bottom-up approach) in transformation of societies.

Maier also emphasizes how Columbia has set records in gender inclusive data of victims of armed conflict and their inclusion in decision making process. She writes, "Colombia's National Centre for Historical Memory (CNMH or the Centre) released its report on the experience of LGBTI persons within the context of the armed conflict titled 'Aniquilar la Diferencia' (Translated as 'Annihilate the Difference') on 27 April 2016." " 'Annihilate the Difference' is an historic report by officially recognising, for the first time, that LGBTI people have suffered the violence of the armed conflict...

On 11 February and 6 March 2015, the members of Colombia's peace negotiation table invited two prominent LGBTI civil society organizations to address a gender subcommittee during their exploration of point six in the peace agenda, victims of the armed conflict" (Maier, 2019). These steps led to exemplary contributions in the field of gender justice and instilled hope for a society grappling with post war anxieties. I shall conclude this essay by underlining the epistemological and practical need for gender centric approach in understanding and analyzing transitional justice. LGBTQI individuals and communities are often targeted in fragile postwar societies in which violence between the formerly warring communities is no longer acceptable and, as such, can easily become submerged in more politically allowable forms of discrimination (Nagle, 2019).

Therefore, there is a need for queer, decolonial, and intersectional analysis and contribution to the field of

transitional and transformative justice to understand and realize the rights, needs and concerns of LGBTQI community and apply them to transitional justice mechanisms. Otherwise, in the absence of such lens, whole category of victims and survivors of sexual, emotional and political harms shall continue to be left out of access to transitional justice procedures and that in turn shall terribly affect the transformation of that society.

## *Works Cited*

Boesten, J., & Wilding, P. (2015). Transformative gender justice: Setting an agenda. Women's Studies International Forum, 51, 75–80. https://doi.org/10.1016/j.wsif.2014.11.001

Carothers, T. (2002). The End of the Transition Paradigm. Journal of Democracy, 13(1), 5–21.

Diamond, L., Fukuyama, F., Horowitz, D. L., & Plattner, M. F. (2014). Reconsidering the Transition Paradigm. Journal of Democracy, 25(1), 86–100. https://doi.org/10.1353/jod.2014.0018

Fobear, K., & Baines, E. (2020). Pushing the conversation forward: the intersections of sexuality and gender identity in transitional justice. Semantic Scholar, 24(4). https://doi.org/10.1080/13642987.2019.1673980

Gready, P., & Robins, S. (2014). From Transitional to Transformative Justice: A New Agenda for Practice. International Journal of Transitional Justice, 8(3), 339–361. https://doi.org/10.1093/ijtj/iju013

Madlingozi, T. (2010). On Transitional Justice Entrepreneurs and the Production of Victims. Journal of Human Rights Practice, 2(2), 208–228. https://doi.org/10.1093/jhuman/huq005

Maier, N. (2019). Queering Colombia's peace process: a case study of LGBTI inclusion. The International Journal of Human Rights, 1–16. https://doi.org/10.1080/13642987.2019.1619551

Nagle, J. (2019). Frictional encounters in postwar human rights: an analysis of LGBTQI movement activism in Lebanon. The International Journal of Human Rights, 24(4), 1–20. https://doi.org/10.1080/13642987.2019.1619550

# IX

# Digital Equality: Addressing the Challenge of Cyberspace Hatred Against Women in ASEAN Doan Nguyet Ha

*Abstract*

The research paper delves into the growing concern of online harassment and hate directed towards women in the ASEAN (Association of Southeast Asian Nations) region. The study employs a comprehensive analysis of the various forms of cyberspace hatred, including cyberbullying, online misogyny, and gender-based violence, with a specific focus on how these issues manifest within the cultural and socio-political context of ASEAN countries. The research explores the impact of cyberspace hatred on women's rights, personal well-being, and their ability to participate fully in the digital sphere. By examining case studies, online trends, and regional dynamics, the paper aims to provide a nuanced understanding of the challenges faced by women in ASEAN regarding online abuse.

Furthermore, the paper proposes a forward-looking approach to address and mitigate cyberspace hatred against women in the ASEAN region. This includes recommendations for policy interventions, legal frameworks, and community-based initiatives aimed at fostering a safer and more inclusive online environment. The research not only highlights the urgency of addressing this issue but also offers actionable insights to empower stakeholders in implementing effective measures to combat cyberspace hatred against women in the ASEAN context.

**Keywords**: cyberspace, hatred, online harassment, women

## Introduction

With more than 400 million internet users and a thriving digital economy, Southeast Asia is a thriving market for social media. With the exception of Laos, Myanmar, and Timor-Leste, every country in Southeast Asia has an internet penetration rate of at least 70%. In 2022, there will be 326.3 million smartphone users in Southeast Asia, with Indonesia and Vietnam leading the way. Southeast Asia's online media sector was estimated to be worth $ 24 billion in 2022. By 2025, when the internet media market in Southeast Asia was anticipated to be worth roughly $ 36 billion, this was predicted to rise even more.

One cannot ignore the influence of social media and how it has changed and is still influencing our lives today. The ubiquitous access to online spaces for opinion and information-sharing has both benefits and drawbacks. It makes it possible to share not only truthful information and well-intended comments, but also false information, offensive and derogatory language, thereby leading to harassment of the users. The encroachment of privacy facilitated by internet-enabled mobile phones have rendered traditional rules of interaction and engagement obsolete. Also, technology has made it possible for a variety of hate crimes and violent acts to become normalized and widely disseminated, reinforcing and maintaining the structural forms of oppression that present in society.

Over the course of the pandemic, global instances of online gender-based violence, which are regarded by all countries as a major problem, have increased. Sexist and misogynistic language is a common occurrence for many women and girls. Many from this demographic have to suffer due to "Online sexist hate speech" since they not only have an offensive or demeaning tone towards the target audience but also resonate with the entire community, which aids in suppressing, denigrating, and isolating them. The accessibility, anonymity and portability of the mobile screen blurs the traditional binaries of subject/object and boundaries of distinct public/private spaces.

Online hate speech suffers from a number of difficulties, some of which are spreading quickly and with a vast population, a garb of anonymity, a difficulty in establishing the competent jurisdiction to assess eventual wrongs of hate speech and difficulty in the removal of hate messages.

The problem of hate speech is already fairly complex, but the Internet and specifically social media as a whole add another layer of complication. The ease and convenience with which hate speech is spread on the Internet is aided by the following factors:

the formation of "echo chambers"

the polarization of groups and the division of the public opinion

the creation of "cyber cascades"

The convergence of all these factors has the effect of speeding up the dissemination of hate speech thereby resulting in a "fragmented public sphere."

Since the perception of cyberviolence is one of mental anguish rather than physical hostility, it is frequently regarded as a non-corporeal crime. Online violence is "less archetypal," and is viewed as inadvertent and generally benign, whereas we are used to viewing offline violence as bad. In fact, technology speeds up or makes crimes against women against women easier. Moreover, online violence can have serious repercussions as shown by a research in which the survivor claimed that every time she viewed content that involved cyber-violence, "her whole body shuddered and winced" as she read the offensive comments.

Women's existence has been directly threatened by online violence and hate speech, and this has changed the environment they live in (for the worse). This is also true for women who do not have access to the internet, who must also deal with the effects of a changed, more sexist world brought on by unregulated online gender-based violence.

The Internet's perils and difficulties, as well as its ungoverned and uncontrollable area, continue to infiltrate the private spheres of millions of individuals. It is challenging to regain lost confidence and trust in particular online services. Instead, online users frequently retaliate by exercising self-censorship or by forgoing services.

## *Problem Statement*

Online platforms, for a long time, have been considered as a suitable place for individuals who struggle with traditional communicative platforms to connect to each other or comfortably be open. These platforms can be a reliable place for women to share their views, contact with friends or update life when there are advanced technologies which help prevent disinformation or cyber bullying to this so-called vulnerable gender. Normally, toxic contents or inappropriate activities on social media will be automatically deleted or suspended to ensure the safety for users.

However, this is not effective enough as females, especially in ASEAN countries, have to face numerous cyber security risks based on their gender identities or expressions. For example, they could be sexually harassed, threatened or disrespected by comments, messages or posts when freely bringing up ideas or uploading pictures of themselves. Inequality issues and exclusion in the peacebuilding and other societal areas can emerge. Thus, it is crucial to make sure that platforms that support gender safety and positive digital participation have clear, rights-based regulations.

Regarding the background of the problem above, we want to analyze specifically why cyber security is important to women, how women are affected by the toxic digital environment and the recommended solutions .

Definition of online hate speech and its perils in general and ASEAN in particular

How is "Hate Speech" in cyberspace different from traditional hate speech?

Some online issues that need further analysis

Various cases of gendered hate speech where justice for victims was not served due to caveats in legislature and judiciary

Legal gaps, inconsistencies and loopholes in laws and regulations of ASEAN and in global context

How can the different stakeholders take action ?

What is the way forward?

## *Analysis*

How and why this issue is impacting ASEAN and to what extent?

Along with increasing access to information technology, human life today is very dependent on the internet. Data shows that in ASEAN countries, the percentage of internet usage has reached 70%, and will continue to grow. Information dissemination has also increased. This information reaches the public, including through social media. Unfortunately, the more massive the use of social media, the violence that occurs on social media is also increasing. One of the violent issues in social media is cyber hatred.

Cyber hatred is violence characterized by contempt for a person or group of people. In this case, women are often the victims. Then, cyber hatred against women, or Cyber Violence Against Women, is included in online gender-based violence. Cyber Hatred appears in various forms, including: hate speech, hacking, identity theft, and stalking and harassment. Furthermore, social media users will flock to liking, commenting on and even spreading the violent content so that it will directly increase traffic visits which will lead to further dissemination of this information. In the context of Cyber Violence Against Women, women are often a vulnerable group that does not have sufficient capabilities to overcome these problems.

Cyber-hatred against women can have disastrous implications for the lives of these women. In this study, women may experience bullying that threatens their mental health. Women can also lose their jobs because they are seen as defaming the place where they work. These things are further exacerbated by digital footprints that cannot be eliminated.

The phenomenon of cyber hatred can be viewed from the socio-cultural conditions, both for perpetrators, victims, social media users and institutions. This is a challenge for social media provider companies to be more selective in responding to incidents of hate speech against women. Apart from that, the government must also always review and study this phenomenon so that it can create conditions for a peaceful social media climate.

## *The relevant stakeholders*

ASEAN
    ASEAN Member State Counties
    Ministry of Information and Communication in ASEAN nations
    Ministry of Women's Empowerment in ASEAN nations
    Internet service provider company

Women internet users in ASEAN

## *How is this issue in some ASEAN countries?*

Malaysia:

Studies have found high prevalence of online hate speech and harassment targeting women, particularly on social media platforms. Common forms include sexist comments, slut-shaming, and threats of physical/sexual violence. Women activists, politicians, and public figures seem to be disproportionately targeted.

Indonesia:

Online misogyny and gender-based hate speech is a significant issue, especially on social media as this country is one of the biggest social media users. Women politicians, journalists, and influencers face coordinated attacks and smear campaigns. Hate speech often takes the form of sexist slurs, body-shaming, and accusations of promiscuity. For example, calling others by abusive langauge or religion insult.

Philippines:

Common tactics include revenge porn, death/rape threats, and coordinated disinformation campaigns. Marginalized groups like LGBTQ+ women and women of color are especially vulnerable. In 2012, the Foundation for Media Alternatives (FMA) in the Philippines launched an initiative to document and map cases of online gender-based violence (OGBV) occurring within the country. As of June 2023, this ongoing effort has resulted in the mapping of 686 OGBV cases.

In countries like Malaysia, Indonesia, and the Philippines, the case mapping has revealed the pervasive and severe nature of online misogyny, harassment, and abuse targeting women from diverse backgrounds. This can reinforce negative social stereotypes and attitudes towards women, further entrenching patriarchal norms and the devaluation of women's voices and experiences. However, in more socially progressive ASEAN nations like Singapore, the documentation of OGBV cases may spark greater public outcry and demands for stronger social safeguards.

In countries with weaker rule of law and limited gender equality protections, such as parts of Indonesia and the Philippines, the OGBV case data could be dismissed or downplayed by political leaders resistant to addressing women's rights issues. Conversely, in nations with more robust democratic institutions, like Malaysia and Thailand, the evidence of online attacks against women in politics and public life may compel policymakers to introduce legislative reforms and content moderation policies.

## *Methodology*

Highlight the methods employed clearly
Qualitative Research using Secondary Data Collection
This research will be conducted in a qualitative method. The approach will be focusing on collecting data from external sources; i.e. government departments, public sector organizations, and other organizations. Some records, census data, social media monitoring, and other kinds of online and media sources will also be considered. The focus will be on seeing how the issue regarding cyber attacks towards women happen in ASEAN countries, and see how the lawsuits in each country try to control or respond to these problems. Then there will be a comparison as well for the lawsuits between countries and try to analyze what differences resulted from different regulations. Hence, we will be able to see and recommend what's best for the future plan.
Qualitative Research using Literature Review
This method is used to help give a broader perspective, from trying to look at researches done in the past and compare them to the current situation.

## *Limitations of the research*

The data found can be biased or distorted due to the partiality of the authorities
Some countries might give limited access to their lawsuits due to national interests
Previous researches might be biased based on who conducted (or even supported) the research

## *Key Recommendation*

### *Establish an International Cyber Court and Governance Framework:*

Create an international cyber court or tribunal: This specialized judicial body would have the authority to establish and enforce global rules and regulations governing online activities and protecting the fundamental rights of internet users, particularly women. It would address the current lack of universally accessible legislative or judicial mechanisms to oversee and safeguard people's rights in the borderless cyberspace.

Develop a comprehensive global governance framework: This framework would involve collaboration between governments, internet companies, civil society organizations, and other relevant stakeholders. It would aim to establish universal standards, laws, and procedures for upholding cyber rights and ensuring online safety, with a strong focus on protecting women from harassment and hate speech.

Ground the governance framework in human rights principles: The framework should be firmly rooted in international human rights law and provide clear guidance on defining and responding to online hate speech, particularly against women. This would help address the current ambiguity and inconsistencies in how online hate is recognized and addressed across different jurisdictions.

## *Enhance Content Moderation and Transparency:*

Mandate more responsive content moderation systems: Social media platforms should be required to make their content moderation processes more effective in addressing user complaints of hate speech, particularly in minority languages across ASEAN countries. This would help ensure that women's reports of online abuse are promptly and appropriately addressed.

Ensure transparency of automated hate detection methods: Platforms should be compelled to make their automated hate speech detection algorithms transparent and open to public review. This would allow for independent scrutiny and help ensure that these systems are fair, accurate, and not biased against women and other marginalized groups.

Increase investment in anti-harassment initiatives: Internet companies should be required to allocate more resources and funding towards developing robust user safety measures and anti-harassment programs, especially during times of crisis or heightened online activity when the risk of cyberspace hatred against women may increase.

## *Reform Hate Speech Laws and Policies:*

Update hate speech laws to recognize gender-based hatred: Existing hate speech laws should be revised to explicitly recognize and address online hatred and harassment directed at women as a violation of their fundamental rights to equality, autonomy, dignity, and full participation in public life.

Adopt a human rights-based approach to cyber justice: The legal and policy framework for addressing online hate should strike a careful balance between protecting freedom of expression and safeguarding individual rights and security, with a focus on empowering and protecting marginalized groups such as women.

Collaborate with stakeholders in developing and implementing policies: ASEAN governments should work closely with civil society organizations, women's groups, and other relevant stakeholders in developing and implementing comprehensive policies and initiatives to combat online harassment and hate against women in the region.

## *Foster Multi-stakeholder Collaboration and Capacity Building:*

Promote greater involvement of diverse stakeholders: Addressing the issue of cyberspace hatred against women in ASEAN will require the active participation and collaboration of a wide range of stakeholders, including governments, internet companies, civil society organizations, and end-users themselves.

Invest in capacity-building for women and marginalized groups: Programs should be developed to empower women and other marginalized groups in the ASEAN region with the knowledge and skills to navigate the online world safely and effectively, as well as to advocate for their rights and seek redress for online abuse.

Encourage knowledge-sharing and best practices: ASEAN countries should facilitate the exchange of information, experiences, and best practices in addressing the unique cultural and sociopolitical challenges surrounding cyberspace hatred against women in the region. This would help foster a more coordinated and effective regional response.

The perception of the internet (and social media platforms in particular) as a democratizing force is one that greatly serves the interests of large internet companies. Nevertheless, when stripped of these lofty goal statements, it becomes clear that the core activities of these businesses involve the exploitation of people for financial gain and the erosion of important democratic fundamental rights. As a result, rights to privacy, dignity, and equality—ironically, even the right to free speech and expression—have been violated.

Cyberspace lacks universally accessible legislative or judicial bodies, such as a cyber court and a government, bureaucracy, police, or parliament, that would oversee people's activities within that space globally and protect users' rights and entitlements. Therefore, it is crucial for addressing the issue that international human rights agencies provide clear guidance on how to define online sexist hate speech and what actions should be used in response to it.

Social media networks need to make their content moderation systems more responsive to user complaints of hate speech in minority languages across all nations. The automatic hate speech detection methods used by social media networks should be made transparent and open to public review. Platform firms must spend more money on anti-harassment initiatives because during the pandemic they reduced expenditure in this area. State parties must change hate speech laws to recognise gender-based hatred as a violation of women's first-order rights to equality, autonomy, and dignity as well as their first-order right to participate in public life in the online-offline continuum of social interactions.

So, in order to protect freedom and privacy rights as well as those of human growth and security, cyber justice should be built on good governance through a human rights-based approach. In addition, it should foster greater involvement and collaboration between states, non-state actors, private consumers, and providers in order to come to consensus on universal standards, laws, and procedures for upholding them.

## *Conclusion*

Online violence and harassment impact negatively on the development of women in ASEAN in lots of aspects and hinder them to access equality and openess to the society. Therefore, cyber security is neccessary and needs to be ensured and promoted by ASEAN's authorities and all individuals with the view to invent a friendly, sustainable, nontoxic and rights- respected for women and girls.

# X

# Unveiling the link between Underwater Explosions and Ecosystem Destruction
# Rishu Ranjan

*ABSTRACT*

Land restoration in the ocean due to underwater explosions is a critical issue that impacts the delicate ecosystem of marine life. This blog post will delve into the implications of underwater explosions on marine lives, the importance of land restoration in the ocean, and potential solutions to mitigate the devastating effects on the environment. Underwater explosions pose a significant threat to marine life, disrupting ecosystems and causing long-lasting damage. This blog post aims to explore the various issues and challenges related to underwater explosions, analyse their impact on marine lives, and suggest possible solutions to mitigate the harm caused.

Underwater explosions generate intense shock waves and acoustic energy, which can cause physical trauma, behavioural disruptions, and ecological imbalances among marine organisms. Immediate effects include barotrauma, hemorrhaging, and mortality, particularly in species with air-filled cavities such as fish and marine mammals. Sub-lethal impacts can lead to disorientation, temporary hearing loss, and altered feeding and mating behaviours. Over time, repeated exposure may result in population declines, disrupted food webs, and habitat degradation. Underwater explosions result in shockwaves that can cause significant damage to marine life.

Marine organisms such as fish, corals, and other sea creatures are highly sensitive to sudden disturbances. The shockwaves can lead to physical injuries, disorientation, and even death among marine species. Land restoration in the ocean is essential to replenish and rejuvenate the damaged marine habitats. Restoring the ecosystem helps to rebuild the natural balance and biodiversity in the affected areas. It is crucial to preserve the marine environment for future generations and maintain the overall health of the ocean.

**Keyword**: explosion, marine lives, ecosystem, nuke, land restoration.

## INTRODUCTION

The underwater world is a delicate ecosystem, teeming with diverse marine life that thrives in balance and harmony. However, the peace and tranquility of this underwater paradise are often shattered by the destructive force of underwater explosions. Whether triggered by human activities like military operations, shipping, or construction, these explosions have far-reaching consequences on marine lives. Explosions underwater can have devastating effects on marine life and the delicate balance of ecosystems. Land restoration in the ocean becomes crucial to mitigate the damage caused by these explosions. These explosions differ significantly from their land-based counter part due to unique properties of water. Surroundings of water does not absorb the pressure like air does; instead it moves with the shockwaves. As a result, underwater explosions transmit pressure with greater intensity over distance compared to surface explosions.

## STATEMENT OF PURPOSE

The detonation of explosives underwater can result in a series of detrimental effects on marine life, including physical injuries, habitat destruction, loss of biodiversity, and disruption of essential ecological processes. This poses a severe threat to the survival of various species and undermines the overall health of marine ecosystems. The force behind underwater volcanic eruption can be immense. The eruption's chemical mix, including chlorine and water vapor, could potentially affect the ozone layer.

## *LAND RESTORATION*

Land restoration refers to the process of halting degradation or rehabilitating degraded land, typically through activities like reforestation, soil conservation, and the protection of natural process. Its goal to enhance biodiversity, restore ecosystem services and mitigate climate change.

Land restoration takes on different dimensions like:

Restoring Coastal Habitats

Coastal areas are critical transition zones between land and sea. Restoring coastal habitats such as mangroves, salt marshes, kelp forests and coral reefs can have a positive impact on ocean health.

Regulating Pollution and Runoff:

Land restoration efforts should include strict regulations on pollution, excess nutrients, agricultural runoff, industrial discharge and plastic waste.

Integrated Approaches:

Its crucial to consider the interconnectedness of land and ocean. Actions taken on land can have direct or indirect effects on marine environment.

Blue Ecosystem Restoration:

Efforts involve restoring and protecting coastal habitats, ensuring sustainable fishing practices, and preventing pollution.

## *UNDERWATER EXPLOSIONS*

It occurs when a significant release of energy happens beneath the surface of water. These explosions can result from various sources like:

Military Activities:

Torpedoes, depth charges and underwater mines are intentionally detonated underwater for military purposes. These can damage enemy vessels, submarines or underwater infrastructure.

Seismic Surveys:

Seismic air guns intense sound waves into the water to map the seafloor and identify oil or gas deposits. These blasts can have far reaching effects on marine ecosystems.

Accidental Explosions:

Accidents such as ship explosions can lead to underwater explosions. It causes both physical damage and acoustic disturbances.

## HOW UNDERWATER EXPLOSIONS AFFECT MARINE ECOSYSTEMS

Underwater explosions, whether for construction, mining, or military purposes, can have far-reaching effects on marine life, ecosystems, and even the climate. These explosions affect the delicate balance of the ocean, leading to land restoration requirements and how they contribute to the creation of cyclones, destruction on mainland, and ultimately global warming.

The shockwaves from underwater explosions can harm marine mammals, such as whales and dolphins, leading to physical injuries and disruptions in their communication and navigation abilities. The explosions can also destroy coral reefs, which are crucial habitats for a diverse range of marine species, leading to a decline in biodiversity. Sediments stirred up by explosions can smother fragile marine organisms like sea grass beds and affect the water quality, leading to a cascading impact on the entire ecosystem.

Underwater explosions can trigger seismic events that have the potential to create cyclones and tsunamis, leading to widespread destruction on the mainland. These natural disasters can devastate coastal communities, causing loss of life, property damage, and long-term economic repercussions for the affected regions. The need for land restoration efforts in the aftermath of such events becomes crucial to rebuild ecosystems and support the recovery of marine and terrestrial life.

Underwater explosions release large amounts of carbon dioxide and other greenhouse gases into the atmosphere, contributing to global warming and climate change. The warming of the oceans can disrupt weather patterns, leading to more frequent and severe extreme events like hurricanes, droughts, and heatwaves. The resulting rise in sea levels due to global warming poses a significant threat to coastal areas, increasing the risk of flooding and erosion.

The impact of underwater explosions on marine life, ecosystems, and the environment at large cannot be underestimated. It is essential for us to recognize the interconnectedness of all living beings and take proactive measures to mitigate the harmful effects of our actions. Land restoration efforts in the ocean are just one step towards ensuring a sustainable future for our planet and all its inhabitants.

## *ISSUES AND CHALLENGES*

Addressing the impact of underwater explosions on marine life from a legal perspective involves several key steps:

1. Strengthening International Conventions: Building on existing frameworks such as the United Nations Convention on the Law of the Sea (UNCLOS) and the Convention on the Conservation of Migratory Species of Wild Animals (CMS), there should be specific amendments or protocols focused on underwater noise pollution and explosions. This includes setting clear limits and guidelines for permissible activities.

2. National Legislation and Regulations: Countries need to develop and enforce national laws that regulate underwater explosions. This can include requirements for environmental impact assessments (EIAs) before conducting any underwater activities, setting up exclusion zones to protect vulnerable marine habitats, and establishing stringent penalties for non-compliance.

3. Environmental Impact Assessments (EIAs): Mandate comprehensive EIAs for all activities that involve underwater explosions, such as military exercises, construction, and resource extraction. These assessments should include detailed analyses of potential impacts on marine life and propose measures to mitigate those impacts.

4. Permitting and Licensing: Implement a robust permitting system for activities involving underwater explosions. Permits should only be granted if applicants demonstrate that they have taken adequate measures to minimize harm to marine life and comply with all relevant regulations.

5. Monitoring and Enforcement: Establish regular monitoring of underwater activities to ensure compliance with legal standards. Use technologies such as underwater drones and acoustic sensors to detect unauthorized explosions and assess their impacts on marine ecosystems.

6. Public Participation and Transparency: Engage stakeholders, including scientists, environmental organizations, and the public, in the decision-making process. Ensure transparency by making data on underwater activities and their impacts publicly available.

7. International Cooperation: Encourage cross-border cooperation to address the transboundary nature of underwater noise pollution. This can involve joint monitoring programs, shared databases, and coordinated enforcement efforts.

8. Mitigation and Remediation Funds: Create funds, supported by fees from permits and fines, to finance research on mitigation technologies and the restoration of damaged marine environments.

By integrating these legal measures, governments and international bodies can create a robust framework to protect marine life from the detrimental effects of underwater explosions, ensuring sustainable use of marine resources while preserving biodiversity.

## *How to Restore the Land of Ocean and Marine Lives?*

Identifying Areas of Damage: Conduct thorough research and analysis to pinpoint specific areas affected by underwater explosions.

Implementing Restoration Techniques: Utilize strategies such as coral reef restoration, mangrove reforestation, and artificial reef creation to rebuild damaged ecosystems.

Engaging Stakeholders: Collaborate with local communities, governments, and organizations to amplify efforts towards land restoration in the ocean.

Monitoring and Evaluation: Regularly assess the progress of restoration projects to ensure effectiveness and make necessary adjustments.

## *How to Balance Ecosystem and Protect Marine Lives?*

Preservation of Biodiversity: Safeguarding the diverse marine species is essential to maintaining a healthy ecosystem.

Regulation of Human Activities: Implementing strict regulations on fishing, tourism, and industrial activities to prevent further harm to marine life.

Sustainable Practices: Promoting sustainable fishing methods and waste management practices to reduce human impact on the ocean environment.

Educating the Public: Raising awareness about the importance of protecting marine life and the role individuals can play in conservation efforts.

## *SOLUTIONS*

To address the impact of underwater explosions on marine life through legal and regulatory measures, the following solutions can be implemented:

1. Adopt Specific International Protocols:

Enhance Existing Conventions: Amend international treaties like UNCLOS and CMS to include specific provisions for underwater noise and explosions, setting clear standards and thresholds for permissible activities.

Develop New Agreements: Establish new international agreements focused specifically on underwater noise pollution, involving stakeholders from multiple sectors.

2. Implement Comprehensive National Legislation:

Draft New Laws: Enact laws that specifically address underwater explosions, requiring environmental impact assessments (EIAs), setting noise level limits, and designating marine protected areas where such activities are restricted or banned.

Update Existing Regulations: Modify existing environmental protection laws to include stricter controls on underwater explosions and their impacts on marine life.

3. Require Rigorous Environmental Impact Assessments (EIAs):

Standardized Procedures: Standardize EIA procedures to ensure consistency and thoroughness, including specific requirements for assessing underwater explosions.

Mitigation Measures: Mandate the inclusion of detailed mitigation plans in EIAs, such as using noise dampening technologies, timing activities to avoid sensitive periods for marine life, and creating exclusion zones.

4. Establish a Permitting and Licensing System:

Strict Criteria: Develop stringent criteria for issuing permits, ensuring that only activities with minimal environmental impact are approved.

Regular Reviews: Conduct periodic reviews of permits to ensure ongoing compliance and adapt to new scientific findings.

5. Enhance Monitoring and Enforcement:

Technological Solutions: Utilize advanced technologies such as underwater drones, acoustic sensors, and satellite monitoring to track underwater explosions and their impacts.

Strengthen Enforcement: Increase funding and resources for enforcement agencies to monitor compliance and impose penalties for violations effectively.

6. Promote Public Participation and Transparency:

Stakeholder Engagement: Involve scientists, conservationists, industry representatives, and the public in the regulatory process to ensure diverse perspectives and expertise are considered.

Transparency Initiatives: Make information about underwater activities, their environmental impacts, and regulatory compliance publicly available to enhance accountability.

7. Foster International Cooperation:

Joint Monitoring Programs: Establish multinational programs to monitor and assess the impacts of underwater explosions, sharing data and best practices.

Harmonized Standards: Work towards harmonizing standards and regulations across countries to prevent regulatory gaps and ensure consistent protection of marine life.

8. Create Mitigation and Remediation Funds:

Funding Mechanisms: Set up funds supported by fees from permits and fines, dedicated to research on mitigation technologies and restoration of affected marine habitats.

Compensation Schemes: Develop compensation schemes for communities and industries affected by stricter regulations, encouraging compliance and support.

By implementing these solutions, governments and international bodies can significantly mitigate the impact of underwater explosions on marine life, promoting sustainable practices while protecting marine biodiversity.

## *CONCLUSIONS*

In conclusion, underwater explosions have a profound and lasting effect on marine lives, posing a significant threat to the delicate balance of underwater ecosystems. By recognizing the issues and challenges associated with underwater explosions and implementing effective solutions. Land restoration in the ocean is a vital endeavour to counteract the detrimental effects of underwater explosions on marine lives. By understanding the impact of these explosions, recognizing the importance of ecosystem restoration, and implementing effective solutions. Restoring the land of the ocean and protecting marine lives are essential actions to maintain the delicate balance of ecosystems. By implementing restoration techniques, engaging stakeholders, and promoting sustainable practices. It is our responsibility to take action and preserve the beauty and biodiversity of our oceans.

# XI

# Nalanda International University: A Soft Power Project Sanjeev Kumar

## *Introduction*

Inauguration of permanent campus of Nalanda University on 19 June 2024 seen as the revival of Nalanda Mahavihara. Nalanda University was established by Kumaragupta in 427CE, 500 years before Oxford University and was the seat of knowledge of the known world, where over 11,000 students from across the globe came for studies. Located at a mere 12 km from the ruins of Nalanda, the new campus of the university has been taking shape over the last four years in Rajgir - a town that is over 100 km from Patna. The Campus is spread over 455 acres, and is complete with academic and administrative blocks, teacher and students living quarters, laboratories and libraries.

With the great efforts of our former President APJ Abdul Kalam in 2005/ 06 the Bihar government passed the bill in the state assembly regarding revival of Nalanda University, it picked up momentum in February 2006 when the former Indian President A P J Abdul Kalam suggested taking up the idea again to his counterpart in Singapore. Since then a partnership of Asian countries, especially Singapore, China, Japan, and South Korea have played active roles in reviving the university. The leaders of Singapore and South Korea, during their bilateral discussions on the sidelines of the second East Asia Summit(2007), decided to support the efforts to revive the university. In 2007 NMG (Nalanda Mentor Group) formed by then Prime Minister of India Dr Manmohan Singh. This Group is headed by the Nobel laureate Amartya Sen. In 2010 , Nalanda Parliament Act passed in Indian Parliament.

## *History and Culture Connection*

Founded in 427 CE, Nalanda is considered the world's first residential university, a sort of mediaeval Ivy League institution home to nine millions books that attracted 10,000 students from across Eastern and Central Asia. Nalanda Mahavihara's multidisciplinary tradition involved lessons in mathematics,astronomy,grammar ,logic and defence studies and above all Buddhist principles at a time when the concept of a university was almost unheard of. It is said to have a 1:8 teacher student ratio, with about 2000 teachers and 10,000 students. This ratio will continue to be maintained in the new campus setting. The ruins of Nalanda University was declared as a World Cultural Heritage site by UNESCO in 2016.

The Dalai Lama said " India is our guru, we are the chelas(disciples), and the source of all the Buddhist knowledge we have, has come from Nalanda".

Nalanda represents the entire Buddhist world and therefore can facilitate cooperation at the much wider geographical scale of Eastern Asia. Nalanda is not simply a historical monument but a living tradition and epitome of culture that fascinated the entire Indian subcontinent, East Asia, South Asia, Southeast Asia and Central Asia over thousands of years. Nalanda disseminated Buddhist religious tradition, especially Mahayana as well as rich material culture will re- integrate these regions in a more friendly manner.

## *People to People Connection:*

Former Singapore foreign minister George Yeo, who was on the University board, said the new Nalanda should be supported by the people living around it like the old Nalanda, "the rebirth of Nalanda is part of the rebirth of Bihar, its development must bring development to the people living around it.

Nalanda University is close to Asia's ancient Buddhist centre of higher education - revival of Oriental languages, study of local issues of the environment, agriculture and livelihood, translation of several manuscripts helps to connect with the people and students . Nalanda has encompassed 200 villages. The University has already identified 60 villages with which it will work to improve livelihoods, promote sustainable agriculture practices to improve productivity, start eco- tourism and impart skills training to the local population. In upcoming years we will see more international NGO(Non Governmental Organisation) working for the development of the people near Nalanda University.

With the opening of Nalanda University, the region around the university will receive more infrastructure development, people around the university will get more opportunities and establish great connections with foreign people .We will see a rise in tourists and this rise brings development for this region . Bodhgaya -Gaya- Nalanda- Rajgir region already receives a large number of tourists from countries like Vietnam, Thailand, Japan, Tibet and more. This region's connectivity will definitely improve.

If we see the data of students coming for study in Nalanda university from different countries is already increasing. In the first intake of 2014, the university received applications from more than 1,000 students from around 40 countries for only 40 seats . For the academic year 2023-24, a total of 187 international students are enrolled, highest from Vietnam, excluding 75 Indian students . Current enrollment in PG and PhD programme for 2023-27 are from Argentina, Bangladesh, Bhutan, Cambodia, Ghana, Indonesia, Kenya, Laos, Liberia, Myanmar, Mozambique, Nepal, Nigeria, Sri Lanka, Republic of Congo, South Sudan, Serbia, Sierra Leone, Thailand, Turkey, Uganda, the USA, Vietnam, and Zimbabwe.

## *Case study of SAU*

The South Asian University (SAU) – an international university established in 2010 by the eight South Asian Association for Regional Cooperation (SAARC) countries – is a unique experiment that demonstrates cooperation in the south Asian region. In a short span of less than a decade, SAU has brought together students from all the eight SAARC countries to study under one roof. When the university started its operations, only a few hundred students applied. But this number has increased significantly over the years, touching around 7,000 for 180 seats in the various Masters courses in 2019. This increasing number of applicants is testimony to the university's success, and its academic reputation. The success of any university is generally measured by the performance of its alumni. The SAU alumni are doing very well. Some teach in leading universities in the south Asian region, some have gone abroad for higher studies in prestigious universities like Oxford, Cambridge, European Central University, and so on. Yet others work in leading think tanks, while some are serving their governments and judiciary.

With the success of the first International University I can say that Nalanda University is also going to become another example. As I highlighted in the previous section that in a less duration of time Nalanda University is already on the path of success. Success of Nalanda University opens gates for other ancient universities like Vikramshila University, Vallabhi University, Mithila University and many more.

## *International Collaboration*

Nalanda University project is greater integration with the East Asian community and attracting foreign investment for local development, especially in infrastructure - Nalanda project the idea of shared culture, shared interests and mutual understanding of the strategic atmosphere in the Asia- Pacific. Inauguration ceremony was attended by 17 countries' Heads of Missions. University conceived as a collaboration between India and East Asia Summit nations.

"Honoured to join other 16 dip colleagues at the inauguration of Nalanda University's new campus. Re-establishment of NU has revitalised civilisation linkages and promoted P2P connect in the region. Will keep our active partnership with NU towards a sustainable Thailand-India relations," Pattarat Hongtong, Ambassador of Thailand to India.

"Front row seat to listen to Honourable PM Narendra Modi ji speak during the official inauguration of Nalanda University. Most impressed. So privileged to visit the UNESCO Nalanda University ruins. Felt very blessed by the spirit of Buddhism," said Singapore's High Commissioner Simon

Wong.

"It also marks the realisation of a longstanding commitment by India to the East Asia Summit grouping. It reflects the seriousness with which we pursue our Act East policy. But most of all, it underlines Bharat's endeavour to emerge as a Vishwa Bandhu, extending the hands of friendship and cooperation to the international community," Jaishankar said during the inauguration ceremony.

"By doing so, we contribute to the rejuvenation of civilisational linkages, to the celebration of our shared cultural heritage, and to the appreciation of the immense diversity of our existence," he added.

Funding:- Australia (1 million USD) is supporting the establishment of dean - level chair of ecology and the environment. Singapore has announced it will design, build and donate a state - of- the Art library, at an estimated cost of up to USD 7 million. China in 2011 announced USD 1 million. Thailand has contributed USD 1,32,000 USD, Laos 50,000 USD.

## Conclusion

Nalanda has a very old Buddhist tradition, the epitome of culture and the soul of ancient academics. I am sure that the Nalanda University project became a game changer for development in Bodhgaya- Gaya- Nalanda- Rajgir region and established very good people to people connections with students of other countries. This region has international recognition because of two UNESCO world heritage sites, Mahabodhi Temple in Bodh Gaya and Nalanda ruins sites in Rajgir. Bihar's 70% tourists both domestic and foreign come in this region. The Nalanda University Asia level project creates a good path for development in the region. After inauguration, we got the news that the Bihar government is working for the Metro Project in Gaya . The Nalanda University project is going to be bigger in upcoming years with more funds from India and other countries. Nalanda University is an international university, so regular visits of delegates and foreign officials put this region in the limelight.

## Works Cited

IPCS special report www.advancedjournal.com

https://www.hindustantimes.com/education/features/nalanda-university-a-quest-to-make-india knowledge-centre-101718859270107.html

https://daijiworld.com/news/newsDisplay?newsID=1201009

https://www.straitstimes.com/asia/reviving-indias-nalanda-university

https://www.nytimes.com/2014/03/24/world/asia/indians-plan-rebirth-for-5th-century-university.html

https://www.hindustantimes.com/india/singapore-for-revival-of-nalanda-university/story-sfkhH5GokoUFxS3qaJZeYP.html

https://www.businesstoday.in/magazine/cover-story/story/nalanda-university-rebuilding-help-revive-india-global-role-135341-2014-01-08

https://www.indiatoday.in/education-today/news/story/nalanda-university-receives-applications-from-1000-foreign-students-199390-2014-07-05

https://www.thehindu.com/opinion/lead/Nalanda-a-soft-power-project/article16151885.ece

https://www.cambridge.org/core/journals/modern-asian-studies/article/abs/looking-west-to-india-asian-education-intraasian-renaissance-and-the-nalanda-revival/072BD01B1598166421651C53ED0ACC23#

https://www.rediff.com/news/report/india-garners-support-for-nalanda-university-at-east-asia-summit/20131010.htm

https://www.bbc.com/travel/article/20230222-nalanda-the-university-that-changed-the-world

https://www.universityworldnews.com/post-mobile.php?story=20130213115825860

https://thewire.in/education/south-asian-university

https://www.firstpost.com/india/5-ancient-indian-universities-that-shaped-global-knowledge-besides-nalanda-13783965.html

# XII
## Uncaring Bianca Faustina Morrison

It's all a haze,
Like a blurry memory—
A fleeting glimpse,
One swipe and gone.
We forget those who have passed on,
Undeservingly.
While we laugh and remain glad on
These platforms,
We don't truly remember,
Nor resonate with their grief.
We are like ignorant thieves,
Keeping quiet selfishly.
Children die,
Parents cry,
Houses shatter.
All this is
Painted like sad glitter
On the apps,
In the articles,
In the voices,
Everywhere.
Our worlds don't collide,

A child's life loses value.
Elsewhere, children freely argue,
While men are made weak,
With broken promises to keep.
We have vision,
Yet we are blind,
Blinded by hope
That everything will restore,
Only to know
That some
Review just what's in store
For themselves, and themselves alone.

# XIII

# Vasudhaiva Kutumbakam and its role in addressing the Global Humanitarian Crisis Suraj Yadav and Kavya Roy Choudhury

*Abstract*

The Hindu scripture Vasudhaiva Kutumbakam, meaning "the world is one family," is a significant concept in India's philosophy. It is so valuable that the Indian parliament building's entrance is etched with its worth. India is among the few nations that uphold the concept of 'Vasudhaiva Kutumbakam India's leaders, ranging from Jawahar Lal Nehru to Narendra

Modi, have explained the country's global view by citing the Maha Upanishad's Vasudhaiva Kutumbakam (the world is one family). All leaders have used this phrase to convey a range of ideas, despite variations in their political and religious views. The expression has grown to be essential to India's humanitarian crises and diplomatic endeavours. This paper focuses on the possible contribution that Indian pharmaceutical companies could make in the future to humanitarian aid efforts in developing countries.

India's cooperation with UN organizations, such as the World Food Programme (WFP) and the World Health Organization (WHO), exhibits its dedication to tackling global issues by providing medical supplies, equipment, and specialists to underprivileged countries and how the principles of "Amrit Kaal" and "Vasudhaiva Kutumbakam" are entwined with India's vision for a successful and united future. This paper focuses on the impact of Vasudhaiva Kutumbakam on the distribution of humanitarian help to nations experiencing hardship.

**Keywords**- Humanitarian, UN organizations, Vasudhaiva Kutumbakam, Amrit Kaal, Global

## *Introduction*

The Hindu scripture Vasudhaiva Kutumbakam is said to mean "the world is one family." It is so valuable that the Indian parliament building's entrance is etched with its worth. The phrase originates from the ancient Sanskrit words kutumbakam, which means "family," and Vasudeva, which signifies the Eternal Reality. Vasudha is an alternative spelling of the word "Earth." The phrase conveys the same general idea, which is that reality, the universe, and the world are all one. India is among the few nations that uphold the concept of "Vasudhaiva Kutumbakam. By imposing forced droughts, controlling river flows, creating debt traps, and altering the air, land, and water borders of its large, medium, and small neighbours, it has no intention of dominating any nation on the planet. It goes back to its own "manava dharma" roots and advances efforts to keep the world peaceful and secure. The idea of one world, one family is at odds with the worsening security conditions globally, not to mention the rising bloodshed in the Middle East. In light of these divisions and mistrust, India's "Vasudhaiva Kutumbakam" philosophy is crucial today.

# *Vasudhaiva Kutumbakam: India's Universal Embraces in Diplomacy and Crisis*

India's leaders, ranging from Jawaharlal Nehru to Narendra Modi, have often invoked the Maha Upanishad's Vasudhaiva Kutumbakam (the world is one family) to elucidate the country's worldwide outlook. The expression has grown to be essential to India's humanitarian crises and diplomatic endeavours. Despite their differences in political and religious beliefs, all leaders have used this phrase to convey a variety of concepts and address a range of issues at various points in time. In 1989, Rajiv Gandhi called upon Vasudhaiva Kutumbakam to contest the idea of the first, second, and third worlds, revive the idea of "One World," and put out the ill-defined notion of an "Earth Citizen." At a 2002 summit of the Asia Pacific Forum's national human rights organizations, Atal Bihari Vajpayee utilised the phrase to claim that "India's understanding and advocacy of human rights are as universal as they are ancient." At the Heiligendamm G8 conference in 2007, Manmohan Singh utilised the phrase to support India's response to climate change and global warming while accepting its worldwide duty. Ultimately, in 2014, in his inaugural speech at the UN, Narendra Modi utilized the opportunity to reiterate India's diminishing argument for Security Council reform and bemoan the failure of the global organization to adequately address cross-border terrorism.

According to the UN Secretary-General If the world is one family, Antonio Guterres claims, it is becoming more and more like a dysfunctional one. The threat of disintegration and eventual conflict is increased by the widening gaps, escalating tensions, and declining trust. Even in the best of circumstances, this division would be quite troubling, but in the current context, it portends disaster.

UN's failure to adjust to a geostrategic and geoeconomics environment that is changing quickly has prevented it from carrying out its purpose. The urgent need for UN changes cannot be ignored any longer, and the process cannot be finished unless the Security Council's makeup is altered to better reflect the realities of the twenty-first century. It would be impossible to ignore India's application to join the Council for very long...India is eminently qualified for permanent membership in the Security Council by any objective criterion, including population, territory, GDP, economic potential, cultural diversity, political system, and past and current contributions to UN activities, particularly peacekeeping operations

Carrying the motto "Vasudhaiva Kutumbakam" (the world is one family), India is striving to overcome the obstacles as "Atma-Nirbhar Bharat," a nation that can stand tall in the world, by ingenuity and self-reliance. People of various faiths have been welcomed into this ancient society, which was founded on Sanatana Dharma. In fact, for ages, the majority community has served as an insulator, mediating religious disputes between other communities.

## India's Global Humanitarian Response Amidst Economic Growth

India's economy was ranked 10$^{th}$ in the world in 2014, however over the past ten years, it has risen to the 5$^{th}$ rank. India has proved its commitment to the Vasudhaiva Kutumbakam ideology by responding to the COVID-19 pandemic. Along with the WHO, India was intimately involved with several other regional organisations, including the African Union (AU), ASEAN, EU, G-20, Quad (a political alliance comprising Australia, India, Japan, and the United States), and SAARC. India supplied medical supplies, equipment, and specialists to over 100 underprivileged countries and demonstrated its dedication and leadership as a BRICS (Brazil, Russia, India, China, and South Africa) member by giving pharmaceutical gifts to 31 nations and engaging in commercial exports to 24 more. To help them weather the COVID-19 pandemic, India has granted grants totalling approximately 85 countries in pharmaceutical aid.

Regardless of two significant catastrophes (the global financial crisis in 2008 and the epidemic in 2020–2022), India has grown at a standard yearly rate of 10.2% in current dollars from 2003–04 to 2022–23. India's GDP is expected to rise from $3.4 trillion in 2022–2023 to slightly over $5 trillion. India would thereafter be in third position, behind only China and the United States. The symbolic impact on India's place in the world order will be enormous. India's position as a first responder in humanitarian matters, "ever-ready to assist the global community in times of need," and the prompt, all-encompassing action taken by the nation during pandemics, floods, earthquakes, and other emergencies.

## *The Guiding Principles of Amrit Kaal for India's Future Development*

An increasingly important concept in India these days is Amrit Kaal, especially when it comes to planning and development for the future. It is a reflection of a bright future for India, focusing on a planned, well-balanced strategy for fostering economic progress. Amrit Kaal was conducted to enhance the quality of life for Indian inhabitants, reduce the gap in development between rural and urban areas, decrease the level of government intervention in citizens' lives, and embrace technology.

In India's vision for a united and prosperous future, the ideas of "Amrit Kaal" and "Vasudhaiva Kutumbakam" are interwoven. As a time of change and advancement, "Amrit Kaal" corresponds with the concepts of harmony, interdependence, and group accountability that "Vasudhaiva Kutumbakam" embodies. The ideal embodied in Amrit Kaal is in line with the philosophy of Vasudhaiva Kutumbakam, which advocates acknowledging our shared destiny and cooperating to achieve common objectives. For India to advance towards becoming a developed and prosperous country, these ideas emphasise the significance of carefully considered plans, balanced scheduling, and coordinated actions.

## *India's Vasudhaiva Kutumbakam: A Legacy of Humanitarian Intervention*

What Indian philosophy may give a contemporary society ripped apart by various conflicts, such as those rooted in racial, religious, and ethnic identities, environmental degradation, and climatic change? Whereas Hebraic culture was commandment-based and God-centered, Indian culture has always been focused on the individual. Muhammad Ghori murdered Prithviraj Chauhan at the first chance, but Chauhan defeated Ghori eighteen times without killing him. This reveals much about the mindset of Indians during warfare. But that doesn't mean we're terrific and that anyone may treat us in any way they choose.

Even Before India was independent and not the richest nation at the time; rather, it was fighting for independence. But still during that time

Maharaja Jam Saheb of the princely state of Nawanagar in Gujrat welcomed Polish women and children as refugees and built a home for them in Balachadi, which the kids dubbed "Little Poland." The Polish government honoured Maharaja Digvijaysinghji Jam Saheb after gaining independence by erecting a monumental Good Maharaja Square and a school bearing his name. There are extremely few people that are aware of this reality. This aims to demonstrate how deeply ingrained Vasudhaiva Kutumbakam has been in Indian culture for many years.

India and the Maldives have recently been at odds, although When the Maldives faced a drinking water crisis in 2014, the Indian Navy dispatched two patrol vehicles and seven transport planes to transfer 200 tonnes of water by air under the Operation Neer humanitarian aid mission. With two reverse osmosis systems capable of producing twenty tonnes of water per day and thirty tonnes of fresh water on board, INS Sukanya placed INS Deepak on standby. In 2017, as part of "Operation Dost," India sent teams of search and rescue experts, together with NDRF personnel, medical supplies, equipment, and a field hospital, to Turkey and Syria. The mission was to give the impacted areas vital assistance and relief. Another example of its prompt outreach to its neighbours in times of distress is Operation Insaniyat, which in 2018 provided humanitarian supplies to both the locals and Rohingya refugees.

Back in 2015 The Saudi-led coalition and Shiite rebels were engaged in a bloody struggle in Yemen, with the erstwhile bastion of President Abedrabbo Mansour Hadi, who had fled abroad, being one of the places they have taken over. 232 citizens of 26 nations, together with the USA, France, Italy, Canada, and the UK, received assistance from India from the war-torn nation of Yemen. Additionally, citizens of Bangladesh, the Maldives, Nepal, and Sri Lanka have been evacuated. India also saved Pakistani people during the operation, even though Pakistan had not requested assistance for the evacuation of its citizens.

The nation's response to world health during the disastrous COVID-19 pandemic was influenced by Vasudhaiva Kutumbakham. Using its humanitarian approach in response to the COVID-19 pandemic, India dispatched groups of Indian military doctors to countries such as Nepal, the Maldives, and Kuwait to assist the national authorities in developing strategies to stop the pandemic's spread. When the COVID-19 pandemic struck, Bangladesh purchased Indian COVID-19 vaccinations after China requested to split the expenditure of the vaccine trials. Afghanistan obtained

500,000 doses of AstraZeneca's COVID-19 vaccine from India in the most recent Vasudhaiva Kutumbakam acts. This was the first time Afghanistan had received COVID-19 vaccinations from any country in the globe.

Ever since the war started, India provided medical supplies and pharmaceuticals to Ukraine as humanitarian help. Consignments of medical supplies, sleeping bags, blankets, tents, generators, and other necessities for supporting schooling in the impacted areas have been sent by India to Ukraine on many occasions. India's backing for the people impacted by the crisis is demonstrated by the substantial humanitarian assistance donations sent to Ukraine by the Indian government and pharmaceutical businesses, amounting to 97.5 tonnes.

Notwithstanding the intricate political circumstances in Afghanistan and Ukraine, India persisted in providing humanitarian aid. India demonstrated its dedication to supporting the Afghan people in difficult times by sending wheat, medications, and other necessities to Afghanistan throughout the year. Consignments of food and medical supplies were also sent to Ukraine, demonstrating India's support for a country that is suffering greatly from the crisis.

India's geopolitical location allows it to interact positively with other power blocs, and its aptitude for navigating tricky diplomatic situations positions it as a possible international crisis mediator. India has developed as a nation of vast diversity and cultural richness, as well as a major actor on the international scene, representing the values of collaboration, peace, and mutual respect in a period marked by rapid changes and complicated challenges. India's historical non-alignment and strategic location allows it to interact positively with many major power blocs. India has demonstrated that amicable ties with nations with different philosophies and systems of government are achievable. This proficiency in navigating convoluted diplomatic seas positions India as a possible international crisis mediator.

To rescue more than 3,000 citizens who were stranded in Sudan due to the proceeding violence, India started Operation Kaveri. Under Operation Kaveri, the Indian Air Force helped over 150 stranded Indians return safely and delivered 24,000 kg of humanitarian material to Sudan. This mission focused on the fallout from the 2021 coup of the Sudanese government, which sparked a bloody civil war. 3,862 people were successfully evacuated during Operation Kaveri, which involved the participation of 17 planes and five Indian Navy ships in a massive humanitarian effort.

India's position on the Israel-Palestine issue has been shaped by its dedication to the ideology of Vasudhaiva Kutumbakam. India has demonstrated a balance between the fundamental values of ahimsa (non-violence) and justice by expressing sympathy for the Palestinian cause and people while simultaneously denouncing violence committed by organisations such as Hamas. India's most recent humanitarian act was sending aid to war-torn Palestine following the opening of the Rafah border crossing between Egypt and Gaza, which allowed much-needed relief to enter the region for the first time since Israel closed it off. A C-17 aircraft of the Indian Air Force took off from Delhi with 32 tonnes of disaster relief supplies and over 6.5 tonnes of medical supplies for the people of Palestine.

## *India: A Key Player in Shaping the Future of Global Health*

Given its current position, India has a great opportunity to significantly impact the future of global health by enhancing global health regimes, promoting fairness for low- and middle-income nations, sharing its knowledge of pharmaceutical innovation and health systems research, and building national resilience to climate change. The globe would become more like one family as a result of these results. India can assist LMICs in adjusting to the health risks brought on by climate change. The need to create a worldwide, cooperative framework for climate adaptation is highlighted by the eminence of health issues at COP28. For this kind of cooperation to occur, gaps must be closed between Western aid and technology and the real requirements of developing nations. India might promote health-related climate adaptation methods by making use of its positive links with the West and the Global South.

Indian pharmaceutical companies may be a major player in the future when it comes to giving humanitarian aid to developing nations. Over the past fifty years, Indian companies have achieved success in both satisfying home demand and securing a prominent role in the global pharmaceutical industry. With Indian products accounting for more than 40% (by volume) of US pharmaceuticals, India already contributes more than 20% by value to the global generics industry. In 1969, worldwide medicines held a 95% market share in India, while Indian pharmaceuticals held a 5% share. By 2020, however, the situation had reversed, with worldwide pharmaceutical sales accounting for 15% and Indian sales for nearly 85%.

As part of its commitment to successfully promoting harmony and cooperation in the face of global problems, India chose "Vasudhaiva Kutumbakam," or "One Earth - One Family - One Future," as the subject for its 2023 G20 Presidency. The G20 Presidency was important because it heralds the start of Amritkaal, the 25-year period that starts on the 75th anniversary of the country's independence and ends on the centennial of that freedom. One of India's top concerns was climate change, as the country looks to technology and climate funding to ensure that developing countries can make the transition to cleaner energy sources.

India's cooperation with United Nations organisations, such as the World Food Programme (WFP) and the World Health Organisation (WHO), demonstrated its dedication to tackling global issues. India's involvement in fostering collaboration on disaster management and humanitarian assistance was emphasised by its active engagement in regional organisations such as BIMSTEC and SAARC. Vasudhaiva Kutumbakam is especially pertinent in the era of globalisation. It stands for social justice, human rights, and the ethical principles of treating every soul with respect and dignity. Vasudhaiva Kutumbakam has significant effects on peace-making, cultural exchange and understanding, environmental consciousness, and conflict resolution.

## *India's HADR capabilities*

India has been known throughout the Indian subcontinent as a "net responder to crisis," helping its neighbours on the continent and in the sea to lessen the crippling effects of climatic catastrophes and natural disasters. When states have experienced natural catastrophes like cyclones and floods, India has given aid and support to its neighbours, Bhutan, Bangladesh, Sri Lanka, and Nepal. Throughout this mission, India has conducted humanitarian relief operations through its major institutions, including the Indian Armed Forces, which are competently led by the Indian Army and Indian Navy and appropriately supported by the Indian Air Force on an international scale, and the National Disaster Response Force (NDRF) at the domestic level.

The Indian Armed Forces jointly conduct HADR, an operational activity, during peacetime. The Indian Navy (IN) is engaged in task disaggregation, reconnaissance, and Search and Rescue Operations (SAR) to aid millions of people in various tsunami-affected countries in 2004, the Indian Navy's (IN) significance in the country's diplomatic toolkit became apparent for the first time.

In 2005 a tsunami devastated a significant portion of Southern Asia, which borders the Bay of Bengal, as well as the coastal region of the South Eastern Indian Ocean. The number of fatalities in the impacted areas surpassed 200,000. This was a multi-national disaster in many respects, affecting countries as far afield as the East Coast of Africa and spanning over the ocean to include Indonesia, Sri Lanka, India, Thailand, Malaysia, and Myanmar. The first Indian navy helicopters arrived in Sri Lanka with relief supplies within 12 hours of the tsunami devastation. The Indian military was able to communicate with Indonesia as well as provide aid to Sri Lanka and the Maldives. India which was affected as well Particularly in the A&N islands, turned down aid from foreign NGOs and nations. India appeared to be capable of handling the disaster, based on both early and later estimations of the tsunami's death toll and destruction. Also, India believed that the other nations in the area were in greater need of this assistance than itself.

To help other regional nations mitigate the effects of natural disasters, India has refused foreign aid during the crisis and used its resources, including naval ships, helicopters, and other relief equipment, to provide humanitarian relief. These HADR operations across Sri Lanka, the Maldives, and Indonesia during the Indian Ocean tsunami allowed India to project its soft power capabilities within the neighbourhood.

Throughout the years, India has employed HADR as a tactic to lessen the effects of calamities in both the Indian Ocean Region (IOR) and South Asia, a region vulnerable to natural catastrophes. To prevent States in its immediate and surrounding neighbourhood from suffering unduly from natural disasters and emergencies brought on by climate change, India has made HADR a top foreign policy objective. This is because climate change has made some States more susceptible to climatic disasters.

Multiple obstacles stand in the way of Vasudhaiva Kutumbakam. Strong differences exist across countries and groups as a result of historical biases, geopolitical unrest, and economic inequality. They have the power to impede the way toward world peace. To address these problems, awareness and education are essential. To break down stereotypes and increase empathy, cultural exchange programs, diversity in the classroom, and intercultural awareness are all important. International accords and diplomatic efforts can aid in bridging divides and promoting important dialogue. Cooperation between nations can be facilitated by giving international bodies more authority and a stronger mandate. Global health problems can be addressed by working together, as demonstrated by programs that promote cooperation in research, technology, and medicine, including the World Health Organization's pandemic response.

## *The Purpose Of The G20*

G20 represents approximately two-thirds of the world's population, 75% of international trade, 80% of the Gross World Product (GWP), and 60% of the world's land area. It was established as a post-World War II drive to ensure international monetary stability and cooperation as well as to convey a variety of other issues with global dimensions. At present, G20 is one of the largest and biggest intergovernmental forums, made up of 19 countries and the European Union (EU). The G20, which is made up of the majority of the world's greatest economies and includes both developed and developing countries, tries to resolve important global economic problems like sustainable development, international financial stability, and climate change mitigation.

In 2023 G2o summit in India was successful in forging a complete agreement on the New Delhi Declaration, which saw a softening of the U.S. and Russian positions in addition to emphasis on the SDGs, climate action, and green development projects. India stressed how urgent it is for vulnerable states to have a quicker debt relief strategy. About climate change, the Delhi Declaration highlighted the need for poor countries to mobilize "$5.8-5.9 trillion in the pre-2030 period" and $4 trillion annually for clean energy technologies by 2030 to meet targets for net-zero greenhouse gas emissions by 2050.

LiFE (Lifestyle for Environment) was highlighted along with the related environmentally sustainable and responsible choices that lead to globally transformative activities that make the future cleaner, greener, and bluer. These choices are made at the level of individual lifestyles as well as national development.

The African Union (AU), stands for 25% of the world's population. In the global group, such a number cannot be left unrepresented. AU has now been admitted as a new G20 member. At full strength, the AU has 55 members; however, six countries ruled by the military are presently suspended. With 1.4 billion inhabitants, it has a $3 trillion GDP overall. Additionally, it was the first time the powerful bloc had grown since its founding in 1999.

The Indian External Minister, S Jaishankar, stated in one of his speeches that "humanitarian crises require a sustainable solution" that provides the most afflicted parties with urgent relief, but that "terrorism and hostage-taking are unacceptable." Jaishankar further asserted that all States must uphold international humanitarian law. Preventing the spread of conflict both within and outside the region is equally crucial.

## Conclusion

To conclude, the notion of Vasudhaiva Kutumbakam is highly pertinent in contemporary times, especially for India, given its involvement in international crisis management, humanitarian endeavours, and global diplomacy. Indian politicians have applied this antiquated mindset, which echoes the notion of the world as one family, to a variety of global concerns, ranging from climate change to humanitarian disasters. India's devotion to Vasudhaiva Kutumbakam is demonstrated by its proactive approach to humanitarian aid distribution to numerous nations, its dedication to global health, and its engagement in international forums like the G20. Moreover, the practical implementation of this ideology is exemplified by India's approaches to disaster assistance, climate change adaptation, and conflict settlement.

The example of India serves as a model of caring, inclusive leadership, despite the difficulties and complexity associated with advancing the notion of one world, one family. With their advocacy of cooperation, mutual respect, and togetherness among variety, the principles of Vasudhaiva Kutumbakam offer a beacon of hope amidst the ongoing global tensions and the emergence of new crises. An integrated and peaceful world is genuinely attainable, as evidenced by the humanitarian initiatives India has left behind and its dedication to influencing global health and economic governance. Education, diplomacy, and cooperative efforts will be crucial in overcoming challenges, fostering trust, and bridging gaps. Vasudhaiva Kutumbakam's vision, bolstered by India's deeds and leadership, has the potential to inspire a more peaceful and linked global community through these activities.

# XIV

# Satyamev Jayate: A Social Mirror TV Show
## Sanjeev Kumar

*Introduction*

A Star India and Aamir Khan production initiative, Satyamev Jayate was a TV show, aired 11 AM every sunday with the first episode on 6 may 2012 and ran three successful seasons. Satyamev Jayate was also simulcast on Doordarshan and other channels and regional channels of Star Network. It was hosted by the Bollywood actor Amir Khan.

Satyamev Jayate was a documentary -cum talk show voiced out strong social messages and touched the lives of many. Each episode presented a social issue that was widely prevalent and backed by extensive research. The issues taken up during each episode stirred up strong emotions among the audiences and brought about a sense of unity. Satyamev Jayate brought to the fore issues such as female foeticide child sexual abuse, rape, domestic violence honour killing, untouchability, alcoholism and of politics - not just by getting different point of views but through numbers that reflected the intensity of this issues and also discussed possible solutions for the same.

According to the data , in the last 30-40 years three crore female foeticide happened in India. Its purpose was to show the light to empower the Indian citizens and make them believe that India needs change, and all of us, together, can make a difference. With the purpose to create hope and positivity, it also empowers citizens with information about their country's social issues and urges them to take action.

## *Public Reactions*

On 6 May 2012, the first episode of Satyamev Jayate aired, taking on a very sensitive issue of our society, female foeticide. The viewer responded with great empathy and support all across the social media channels, along with an enthralling response from eminent personalities. With the first episode watched by nearly 6 crore Indians, that is, two out of every three Indians who watch television had Seen the show. The show garnered 4 TVR(television viewership ratings) in the Hindi speaking market (HSM) for cable and satellite (C&S) audiences in the four years -plus group, and a 4.9 TVR for all HSM including C&S and terrestrial homes for the first episode.

It also caught the attention of social media users with Satyamev Jayate the top trending topic in India on Twitter ( currently X ) on the launch day. Eight out of ten trending topics in India on 6 May 2012. Altogether, there were 968,86,902 Twitter impressions for female foeticide. As per data released by television audience measurement(TAM) media research, Satyamev Jayate launched an episode of the second season watched by 7.9 crore Indians. Star India also claims that the online fan community has doubled from 1.6 million last season to 3.6 million this season. YouTube recorded 17 million views over the show's 13 episodes. Zee Marathi or other regional channels also talk of a selected issue more closely.

## *Comparison with Other TV Show:*

Before Satyamev Jayate few more shows came, which show the issues that exist in our society. Shows like Rajani in 1985, Crime Patrol in 2003, Aap Ki Kachehri with Kiran Bedi in 2008, and Savdhaan India in April 2012 already came, but failed to reach mass audiences in both rural and urban areas because the reach of television is limited and presented in a fictional manner. Satyamev Jayate on the other side's main strength was real people with real stories. The show starts with an interview after introducing the guest in a small video clip, after that talk with other suffering people, showing real data with graphs and maps, and messages make this show special. This show was dubbed in eight different regional languages , shown in 100 countries. All of which are first for any Indian TV show. No other talk show had such reach or was designed to be viewed by the whole country in this manner. There will be a follow up column in Hindustan Times written by Aamir Khan on each issue, every Monday, day after the show. And a follow up segment on Star News every Friday on audiences feedback, response, impact and account of action taken on every issue taken up previous Sunday.

## *Positive Impact of The Show:*

Satyamev Jayate was the show which literally became the talk of the town. The official site of Satyamev Jayate crashed within minutes after the telecast of the first episode and a hundred thousand people dialled in to talk to the host and show their support. It made them believe in the power of change and encouraged them to act for the betterment of the society. At the end of the first episode Amir Khan requested the people to write a letter to the Rajasthan High Court and demand the setting of a fast track court to ensure speedy justice to the victim of female foeticide. Rajasthan High Court immediately set up a fast track court to hear plea related to female foeticide.

Within a year of setup 31 convicted for violating the Pre -Conception and Prenatal Diagnostic Techniques (PCPNDT). The Rajasthan government also carried out 20 sting operations in 2012 and 2013 and cancelled licences of 150 centres and many doctors. The Rajasthan government started the "Waste Free Jodhpur" campaign for a healthier and cleaner society. The Indian Parliament standing committee invited the team of the show to discuss the issue after second episode on child sexual abuse. The bill concerning the protection of children from sexual offences was passed from the lower house of the Parliament . The bill name was Gender Neutral Bill passed for both boys and girls.

After the second episode, the child helpline 1098 was extended to 291 districts. A one -stop crisis centre (OSCC) called Gauravi was inaugurated at A hospital in Bhopal. This centre helps rape victims to register complaints, get medical treatment and services among others. The City office of the child helpline has seen about half A dozen cases since the second episode. 267 calls reporting of molestation and 529 reporting rapes were recorded , an increase from mere 44 and 93 calls respectively. Many other state governments also take action after the show. Madhya Pradesh Health

Department suspended the licences of up to 65 Medical Termination of Pregnancy Centres, therefore putting a stop to even the opportunity of the crime.

The Haryana government announced that pregnant women would have to submit their identification and necessary documents before testing the sex of babies at Ultrasound. The Maharashtra government announced that generic medicines will be made available in government hospitals,government aided medical stores will be set up across the state. This was the effect of the fourth episode. The Madhya Pradesh government began conducting free medical tests and distributing free medicines. The Health Minister of Bihar had invited Aamir Khan to support his Bitiya Bachao (Save Girls Child) campaign.

## *Controversies*

Satyamev Jayate was also part of many controversies. Many allegations were labelled on the show regarding theme song copyright, advertisements, and Aamir Khan production house. The critics also say that Aamir's Satyamev Jayate fails to show a mirror to the society. It was alleged that the donation money from Satyamev Jayate was issued for masjid construction assistance. It was alleged that Aamir Khan production house charged three crore per episode and also said that Aamir Khan showed false sympathy in the show for the victims.

## *Today Challenges in The Society:*

The Satyamev Jayate show ended after three successful seasons. But this show is relevant in today's scenario also because today's society is not different from what it was in 2012. Today's society still has so many issues but incentives like this create space to talk about the issues and understand the society's evil, work to find solutions regarding these issues. According to the caste census data of 2011, the child sex ratio in 2011 was 914/1000. If we compare today, it is 933/1000 in 2022-2023. We still have a difference of 67 girls per thousand boys. We still have a long way to go on this issue. This is not about the single issue that our society is facing. There are so many issues like domestic violence, poverty, education, climate change, dowry and rape. If we see the data then we understand how our society is becoming worse for womens.

According to National Commission for Women(NCW) data, nearly 30% of married Indian Women face domestic violence. Total 28,811 complaints of crimes against women received in 2023, over 50% from Uttar Pradesh. In this 6,274 cases of domestic violence and 4,797 of dowry harassment. According to NHRC( National Human Right Commission) , the total number of complaints registered in 2023 of Child Sex Abuse Material (CSAM) was 4,50,207. We see a rise in these cases , in 2022 it was 2,04,056. In 2023 , total number of rape and attempted rape cases was 1,537. I can surely say that there are so many unregistered cases also and due to society pressure never get registered. This above data shows the face of society, which we all are part of. If we add more data about poverty, death due to dowry and inter-caste marriage, education and climate change then we definitely say the society in which we live is not favourable for all and we need to talk and introspect about these issues.

## Conclusion

We can definitely say that the show has truly been instrumental in raising awareness about the glitches in our society while recognizing the efforts of diverse institutions, NGOs and individuals working for the welfare of the nation. People cannot change in a day and no one can change anything if we are not part of it. But if the future of our nation understands the difference between right and wrong, we are somewhere
heading the right path. This TV show only acts as a mirror of our society. We need to work together for the betterment of our society. Other shows only show fictionalised reconstruction of original cases. Whereas this show has shown only real people talking about their issues themselves. So those comparing it to the likes of Crime Patrol are only belittling their own intelligence. 'Satyamev Jayate' is not just a show, it's a movement to change people's mindset.

## Works Cited

https://globalvoices.org/2012/06/11/
india-aamir-khans-tv-show-stirs-up-social-issues/
https://participedia.net/case/1449

https://lifebeyondnumbers.com/satyamev-jayate-impact-india/

https://www.reddit.com/r/india/comments/occix5/opinion_satyameva_jayate_was_a_ great_show_that/?rdt=47677

https://www.financialexpress.com/archive/aamir-khans-satyamev-jayate-truth-and- dare/1235469/

https://www.slideshare.net/slideshow/analysis-on-satyamev-jayate-research- report/55849116

https://www.businesstoday.in/magazine/features/story/why-advertisers-are-happy-with-satyamev-jayate-33273-2012-08-20

https://urbanasian.com/whats-happenin/2012/05/the-success-of-satyamev-jayate/

https://www.mxmindia.com/media/satyamev-jayate-the-good-the-bad-and-the-ugly-truths-of-life/

https://anujdaga.blogspot.com/2012/05/on-satyamev-jayate.html

https://www.moneylife.in/article/the-truth-about-satyamev-jayates-donations/26553.html

https://reflectionsvvk.blogspot.com/2012/07/it-is-with-considerable-degree-of.html

https://www.disneystar.com//join-our-journey/we-connect/how-ogilvy-and-star-mobilised-people-to-bring-about-change/

https://www.livemint.com/Opinion/rK5bBpGaSbPj3ntsD4FwzN/Sevanti-column.html

https://qrius.com/satyamev-jayate-an-impact-analysis/

https://www.afaqs.com/news/media/42100_satyamev-jayate-ringing-in-change

https://www.news18.com/news/india/satyamev-jayate-the-impact-of-aamir-khans-show-473601.html

https://www.firstpost.com/living/review-aamir-khan-and-satyamev-jayate-failed-in-their-responsibility-1415843.html

https://www.researchgate.net/publication/263203867_Satyamev_Jayate_Return_of_the_Star_as_a_Sacrificial_Figure

https://timesofindia.indiatimes.com/entertainment/hindi/bollywood/news/aamirs-satyamev-jayate-in-copyright-controversy/articleshow/13020122.cms

https://www.business-standard.com/india-news/nearly-30-of-married-indian-women-face-domestic-violence-shows-data-123051400486_1.html

https://timesofindia.indiatimes.com/city/delhi/after-rise-in-21-domestic-violence-cases-fall-in-23/articleshow/106559258.cms

https://www.hindustantimes.com/india-news/nhrc-issues-advisory-regarding-child-sexual-abuse-material-on-internet-101698473197792.html

https://timesofindia.indiatimes.com/india/28811-complaints-of-crimes-against-women-received-in-2023-over-50-pc-from-up-ncw-data/articleshow/106453699.cms

https://www.moneycontrol.com/news/trends/features-2/-1932443.html

https://www.indiaforums.com/forum/topic/2966969

https://www.indiantelevision.com/television/tv-channels/gecs/satyamev-jayate-back-for-season-ii-with-a-difference-140128

https://www.zdnet.com/article/will-social-tv-show-satyamev-jayate-revolutionize-online-television-in-india/